Praise for *Leading Through Collaboration*

Educational leaders who hope to foster the shared vision, collective commitments, and collaborative cultures of true learning communities in their schools will require new ways of thinking and new skills. Leading Through Collaboration *represents a useful resource for those leaders. John Glaser offers a comprehensive set of tools leaders can use to facilitate powerful processes that help diverse constituencies generate and own solutions. Contemporary educators know what it is like to be adrift in a storm of seemingly competing interests and conflicting personalities. Glaser provides them with a compass.*

Richard DuFour
Educational Author and Consultant

If you are in a leadership position, or plan to be, Leading Through Collaboration *will speak to you personally! I can't remember the last time I read every single page of a book, much less every single word. Glaser is a gifted communicator and he has a wealth of knowledge and experience to share with anyone who wants to be a more effective leader. What a marvelous blend of theory and practice! Glaser's writing is so engaging, so personal, and so informative that you will want to read every word. This book should be required reading for every person who is serious about learning how to lead.*

Leonard Pellicer
Dean, College of Education and Organizational Leadership
University of La Verne, CA

This book promises to set a new standard for books on leadership. Written by a very successful leader, problem solver and negotiator, it combines a strong rationale for its practices, well delineated practical strategies, and vignettes from Glaser's extensive background that provide the reader with a clear understanding of how to become a truly collaborative leader.

Pat Wolfe
Education Consultant
Mind Matters, Inc.

John Glaser, one of the foremost practitioners and trainers in organizational problem solving, has finally put his knowledge and experience into a book. Leading Through Collaboration *is essential reading for any manager seeking to lead a collaborative, solution-oriented organization.*

Arne Croce
City Manager
San Mateo, CA

Leading Through Collaboration *is both a comprehensive resource guide and a working manual that will take you to a new level of communication and problem solving. This comprehensive resource manual successfully equips and walks readers step-by-step into and through the most difficult problems they might possibly encounter. The clarity of Glaser's thinking as he unravels and reweaves the recipe for effective communication and problem solving is transformative. Glaser has pulled out tools and compiled them into a systematic, well organized, and user-friendly resource.* Leading Through Collaboration *sets a new standard for communal exploration, openness and authenticity. It articulates concepts and practices that inspire and instruct the reader to move beyond the status quo and into a higher place for the common good of all.*

Sandra Friedman
President Emeritus
Association of Humanistic Psychology

Glaser has packed this book with tools and approaches to deal with every kind of conceivable challenge—from dealing with employees and labor relations to community and governing board issues. Finally, a management book that successfully translates theory into tangible practical applications. The use of public sector examples makes it easy for public sector leaders to identify just how to put the ideas to use in their everyday work lives. A must-have book for public sector managers.

Jim Nantell
City Manager
Burlingame, CA

I love this book! It is practical, readable, and wise, and makes an important contribution to our field. He has done a wonderful job of BOTH describing the underlying theory of his approach AND offering an effective translation into practice. His many helpful examples serve to bring all of his concepts to life. This book is a must-read for anyone who aspires to be a top-notch leader in today's world.

Janet Walden
President and CEO
Center for Collaborative Solutions

Leading
Through
Collaboration

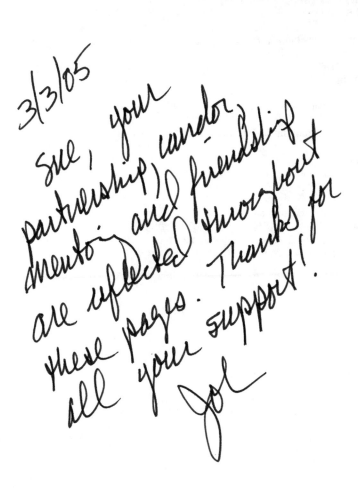

3/3/05

Sue, your partnership, candor, mentoring and friendship are reflected throughout these pages. Thanks for all your support!

Joe

For information:

Corwin Press
A Sage Publications Company
2455 Teller Road
Thousand Oaks, California 91320
www.corwinpress.com

Sage Publications Ltd.
1 Oliver's Yard
55 City Road
London EC1Y 1SP
United Kingdom

Sage Publications India Pvt. Ltd.
B-42, Panchsheel Enclave
Post Box 4109
New Delhi 110 017 India

Printed in the United States of America

Library of Congress Cataloging-in-Publication Data

Glaser, John (John P.)
Leading through collaboration : guiding groups to productive solutions / John P. Glaser.
     p. cm.
Includes bibliographical references and index.
ISBN 0-7619-3806-0 (cloth) — ISBN 0-7619-3807-9 (pbk.)
    1. Group problem solving 2. Conflict management.
3. Organizational behavior. 4. Consensus (Social sciences) I. Title.
HD30.29.G58 2005
658.4'036—dc22

2004018166

This book is printed on acid-free paper.

04   05   06   10   9   8   7   6   5   4   3   2   1

Acquisitions Editor:	Rachel Livsey
Editorial Assistant:	Phyllis Cappello
Production Editor:	Diane S. Foster
Copy Editor:	Michael L. Hoffeditz, Publication Services
Typesetter:	C&M Digitals (P) Ltd.
Proofreader:	Libby Larson
Indexer:	Naomi Linzer
Cover Designer:	Michael Dubowe

Leading Through **Collaboration**

Guiding Groups to Productive Solutions

JOHN GLASER

CORWIN PRESS
A Sage Publications Company
Thousand Oaks, California

Contents

Preface

I have a vivid memory of a chance encounter with a maintenance worker on a high school campus who was chest-deep in a hole where complicated plumbing valves had been uncovered. He was reading intently from a ponderous technical manual he had spread out on the ground in front of him. I've often thought about him over these many years working with a wide variety of entities in the area of organizational development, problem solving, conflict, and change. When we have a thorny mechanical problem to address, we're very comfortable dragging out the manual and figuring out a way to fix things to make them run better. But when we have a sticky organizational or interpersonal problem on our hands, there are few manuals to open or technical support lines to call that give us a handle on how to proceed to make things right.

This book is intended to be such a resource. While I wouldn't advise waiting until a meeting or relationship is raging out of control before opening these pages, they are intended to give individuals and groups support in the process of aligning themselves to work together more effectively to solve problems and address conflict. It includes an inquiry-oriented focus that, when done well, will lead the problem solvers to learn and discover together. This project includes at its core a fundamental belief that anyone in the workplace can and should develop attitudes and skills that will align the organization around learning, which will lead to results that are more productive and satisfying. For this reason, when I refer to a *leader* in the pages that follow, I am thinking not of the head of an organization, department, family, or team, but anyone with the motivation, honesty, and courage to describe, without blame, the problems or situations that need to be changed and to put in motion a search for better ways of doing things. The book is designed to support that process, and this preface is intended to help readers navigate these pages well according to their own learning style.

Much of the experience and passion that I bring to my work with public and nonprofit organizations is reflected in these pages. The creation of *coherence* is by nature a community-building process, which is the very essence of the work done by leaders in schools, cities, counties, and other local governmental entities whose mission it is to deliver excellent services for the public good, whether it is education, public safety, community planning and development, recreation, sewage treatment and disposal, or water. It seems only reasonable that we would attempt to provide those services in a way that creates community in the process. I also hope it will be apparent that creating community is a critical byproduct in any kind of organization in which the key stakeholders expect to have strong relationships with colleagues, bosses, subordinates, customers, neighbors, family members, and even pets. If we can "tune in" to aligning principles, we can harness energies for continually producing agreements that we otherwise might only manage to randomly achieve by luck.

When I began this book, I was working as a consultant and an associate professor of Organizational Leadership. While still in the middle of writing, I assumed the role of superintendent of the Napa Valley Unified School District. So I bring the dual perspectives of support provider and practitioner to these pages, and I draw on examples from each to illustrate these tools and attitudes. I offer them here not as the final answer in how things should be done, but rather as a work very much in progress that represents opportunities for learning that are at the heart of this work.

After many years exploring the potential of leadership through collaboration, I have learned that there are some attitudes that differ from the way most of us have learned to respond to problems and conflict in our lives and in the workplace. In fact, there are some powerful and subtle principles at work in the world that can give us an edge as we work with others to get better results when we address the thorniest problems. Understanding these principles will increase the likelihood that the skills that follow can be applied successfully over time. For this reason, the reader is encouraged to read Part I carefully, for it describes the attitudes that can ensure more successful collaborations. These chapters provide a framework for understanding the personal learning that is a necessary part of this process and they describe how to equip oneself with the attitudes that make generative engagement with others possible.

Readers who by nature want to try a new appliance before reading the instructions may be tempted to go straight to Part II. The chapters in this section are intended to provide a basic set of practical problem solving skills that can make collaboration a reality for users with hands-on problems. This portion can be used as a field guide to provide approaches for organizing people to move through a problem more expediently, as well as ideas for how to work with a team to expand the capacity of its members to collaborate to produce better agreements and to respond proactively to the stressors of conflict and change. If the tools in Part II offer some transitional improvement to the way we approach conflict, the attitudes in Part I include a potential for transformational change that can alter the way we interact with one another.

The index and the sidebars have been designed to cross-reference tools and applications in areas of particular interest and to make it easier for a reader to navigate freely throughout the book.

Taken as a whole, this book is intended to present the rationale for why collaboration taps into powerful forces that can make the world a better place, as well as to provide ample knowledge and practical skills to empower those who want to try.

Acknowledgments

I am indebted to many individuals who have influenced my understanding and practice of collaboration over many years. This includes coworkers and board members of the Napa Valley Unified School District, who have valued, supported, and encouraged organizational learning, and to those individuals in client organizations who have allowed me to accompany their journeys in search of more effective ways of interacting, negotiating, and solving problems. Friends and colleagues at the Center For Collaborative Solutions (formerly the California Foundation for the Improvement of Employer-Employee Relations), and the Department of Organizational Leadership at the University of La Verne encouraged and incubated many of the attitudes and approaches discussed within.

There are a number of people who supported me directly on this project. Jim Nantell, Sandy Friedman, and Barbara Boone each read the entire manuscript and provided invaluable feedback on both the content and the form of this project. Leonard Pellicer, Pat Wolfe, and Eran Mukamel offered support and/or important technical expertise. Rachel Livsey of Corwin Press nurtured and encouraged this endeavor from the very beginning to its completion.

A book on coherence is also necessarily a family affair. My wife, Carol, not only read and critiqued the book, but also collaborated on every idea that it contains. My daughters, Amelia and Bronwyn, each contributed in significant ways to the production of the book as well as my personal education around collaboration and problem solving. Finally my parents, Barbara and Joe Glaser, guided their children to live their lives and interact with the world in a way that would recognize and utilize the potential for coherence.

The contributions of the following reviewers are gratefully acknowledged:

Sue Fettchenhauer
Educational Consultant
Los Gatos, CA

Karen M. Dyer, Ed.D.
Manager, Education and
Non-Profit Sectors
Center for Creative
Leadership
Greensboro, NC

Susan B. Koba, Ph.D.
Project Director
Urban Systemic Program
Omaha Public Schools
Omaha, NE

Marti Richardson
Past President
NSDC
Knoxville, TN

Edie L. Holcomb, Ph.D.
Visiting Professor
University of Louisville
Louisville, KY

Steve Hutton, Ed.D.
On loan to the Highly Skilled
Educator Program
Kentucky Department of
Education
Villa Hills, KY

About the Author

 **John Glaser** is Superintendent of the Napa Valley Unified School District in Napa, California. He was the founding partner of Glaser and Associates, a consulting firm focusing on effective interpersonal learning in individuals and organizations. Throughout his professional life he has explored the nature of dynamic leadership and how people come together to produce more powerful outcomes. His consulting experiences have included a general focus on organizational development, as well as specific training, mediation, and facilitation work with joint labor-relations initiatives. Glaser was formerly an associate professor of Organizational Leadership at the University of La Verne in La Verne, California. He received his doctorate in education from the University of California, Berkeley. He can be contacted at jglaser@prodigy.net.

*This book is dedicated to my wife, Carol, who has
long mentored and nurtured my understanding of collaboration.*

PART I

Staying on One Page: An Attitude of Coherence

Becoming an effective problem solver, collaborator, and consensus builder involves replacing old adversarial and competitive habits with attitudes that maximize the potential for collaboration and teaming. The chapters in this section describe the need for an aspiring problem-solving leader to manage the basic human instincts for fight and flight through responses that will be more conducive to producing agreements in groups in our complex modern world. An understanding and practice of these attitudes is a prerequisite for meaningful success with the skills and techniques described later in this book.

CHAPTER ONE

Coherence

The Mysterious and Scientific Side of Problem Solving

PONDERING ALIGNMENT IN TEAMS

After spending so many hours of my life in meetings, classes, negotiations, and workshops that have either been spectacularly fruitful or numbingly unproductive, I began to look for the patterns and similarities at work when things go well. I noticed that there is an alignment that takes place in a successful group interaction in which the participants seem to build on each other's energy, and share a unity of purpose and a creative synergy that almost seems to guarantee success for an enterprise.

I began to realize at some point in the inquiry that it is possible to use these principles of alignment to become a more powerful and effective problem solver and leader. This "energy" I was perceiving seems to be a common factor in any creative process in which two or more individuals come together to collaborate, that is, to work together to solve a problem or create something new. The term *coherence* implies a phenomenon that can be perceived from group discussions as the thinking of participants begins to form observable patterns. As I will explain later in the chapter, I am borrowing the term from other disciplines to describe the condition that exists when individuals are aligned on a given subject or task, and are ready to harness their collective energy to move forward on a common ground solution.

I have noticed in team building workshops that participants describe this phenomenon when they are asked to specify a great team on which they took part, and to name the qualities that made that team effective. Invariably they would talk about a particular chemistry, based on such qualities as:

- Joint commitment to shared goals
- Trust of all members to understand their roles and get the job done
- Shifting leadership based on task and circumstances
- Excellent communications
- Understanding each other's needs and perspectives
- A sense of humor
- Willingness to set aside differences and to work together for the greater good

None of these qualities separately suggests an unusual alignment or dynamic, but the combination of the characteristics implies that there is something happening that causes each individual to let go of his or her own view of the world in order to become part of something bigger and broader. As we will explore later in this book, letting go is not always a positive thing, but when it happens in the context of a joint effort to create something new that elegantly addresses our greatest needs, it makes it possible to accomplish things that we could never do on our own.

WHY COHERENCE MATTERS

Public sector leaders might well wonder why they should invest precious time and energy learning to perceive and harness the dynamics of coherence in group problem solving and decision making. An answer can be found in the current era of high-stakes accountability that has public educators feeling as if they are continually under siege. A look at current literature suggests that the hope for maintaining the vitality of public education may lie in the ability of educational leaders to successfully cultivate agreement in groups.

Fullan (2003) points out that deep and sustained change in an educational organization can only come to pass when there is broad ownership of the change on the part of teachers and principals. Fullan characterizes the need for leaders to find ways to establish and support "informed professional judgment" that "must be pursued continually through cultures of interaction inside and outside the school (p. 7)." That means that a primary task of the school leader is to "create and sustain disciplined inquiry and action on the part of teachers." He asserts that principals who are not equipped to facilitate this alignment will not be successful.

Lindstrom and Speck (2004) declare that effective staff development programs, the very lifeblood of school reform, "must be founded on a sense of collegiality and collaboration" (p. 15). They describe the "richness" that comes from colleagues inquiring together, innovating to develop new practices, and reflecting together on those practices to create "a new form of professionalism that clearly links leading and learning." They believe that this creates a necessity for principals to lead from within, rather than imposing from above. Similarly, DuFour and Eaker (1998) characterize "collective inquiry" as "the engine of improvement, growth and renewal in a professional learning community" (p. 25).

But despite its current appeal, collaboration and collegiality do not happen spontaneously. As we will see, it requires habits and a discipline that obligates a public leader to be much more facilitative and far less directive than our learned practice may have been.

THRIVING IN AN ADVERSARIAL WORLD

We live in an adversarial world, a fact that is apparent to most leaders whose task it is to create community. Ours tends to be a competitive, blameful society with organizations increasingly subject to customers and coworkers who are determined to get their own way. Often those who most articulately espouse the values of collaboration in working relationships unwittingly revert to fight and flight habits, which have been programmed into our gene pool for tens of thousands of years. While those adversarial habits may be critical to us in a life or death situation, they can also run counter to harmonious principles that could make it much more productive to align disputing parties toward agreement rather than submitting to fight-or-flight.

A Natural Inclination to Be Adversarial

Controlling the extent that we yield to our fight and flight responses is not an easy task. A look at the anatomy of the brain explains why. Emotional pathways in our brains are mediated by the almond-sized amygdala that sits at the base of the brain. As LeDoux (1996) explains it, the emotional responses of the amygdala occur more rapidly and imprecisely than the more "detailed and accurate representations (that) come from the cortex" (p. 165), and so our bodies program us to respond quickly to conflict or perceived danger in a way that prepares us to run or do battle, rather than engage the source of our stress through problem solving. This is a result of the evolutionary processes of natural selection in which our species "learned" that a fight and flight response to danger was the most successful one to keep us from becoming the quarry of natural predators. So while we come equipped with the sections of the cerebral cortex that give us the ability to process sensory information and to respond with conscious complexity, we must be aware that we have an emotional response mechanism that will mobilize us more quickly, and often less reliably (LeDoux, 1996; Wolfe, 2001; Dickmann & Stanford-Blair, 2002).

I experience this conditioning when I'm hiking or running along a road or trail, and I see something snakelike lying in the path. It may be a stick, a piece of hose or tire, or even a dead snake, but my body reacts as if it sees the real thing and I can feel the adrenalin start to rush until my more rational mind takes over and reassures me that there is no danger. Similarly, in my professional and consulting life, I have often worked with teams in which emotion had become so extreme that it was dominating interpersonal interactions. One elementary school faculty was so impacted by emotion that interactions among staff were characterized by shouting, name-calling, and interpersonal avoidance. The result was a toxic environment in which the quality of the services to students was suffering.

A Different Kind of Leadership and Listening

The complexity of modern society and organizations requires a different kind of leadership. We used to rely on charismatic heroes, epitomized in the Hollywood Western by Gary Cooper or John Wayne, to identify what needed fixing and to resolve it quickly with a steady hand and a sure shot. But the world is a more intricately, interconnected place than it used to be, and it is demanding different kinds of leaders who can mobilize the whole team to respond to stressors harmoniously enough to be able to collaborate together on solutions.

The problem solver of the new millennium needs the ability to listen to an open and honest conversation for meaning, intent, and common ground, much as an aficionado of a certain style of music can hear nuances in a piece from that style that are beyond the notice of a less trained ear. It is possible to learn to listen to the "music" of conflict in the same way, and hear patterns and themes that otherwise go undetected. This trained ear enables the problem solver to integrate multiple perspectives in a way that produces something greater than could have been achieved alone.

I had heard over the years about the close connection between jazz and problem solving, but I never truly appreciated this relationship until my brother threw himself a birthday party and hired a jazz duet to entertain. A friend of his, a flute player who lived across the country, came to the party and joined the hired musicians for a large portion of the program. I knew little about jazz, but marveled at how well they worked together and how seamlessly they moved back and forth, one of them improvising while the others played supporting roles. I understood even then that I was seeing collaboration at its best as roles shifted and the leadership changed. The result was delightful music. I was so impressed by how well they played together that I asked the flutist afterwards when they had found time to rehearse. He thanked me and laughed, "Oh, there was no chance to rehearse. I just got up and we started playing." Each of them knew the music well enough and had a well-trained ear for jazz, so that when they started to play together good things just happened.

This phenomenon is not unusual in the jazz world. In fact, the vocabulary that describes the process of playing jazz is rich with the kinds of words that describe the process of problem solving. The language of jazz becomes a helpful way to understand the kind of coherence that gets other kinds of problems solved as well. This collection of quotes from the Jazz School Lucerne (2002, pp. 1–7) conveys that collaborative language of jazz:

It's really just based on listening . . . more than anything else. (Kenny Barron)

When I'm listening to the other musicians and thinking about the form of a piece . . . little things arise which I have to negotiate. (Chuck Israels)

You want to achieve that kind of communication when you play. When you do, your playing seems to be making sense. It's like a conversation. (Tommy Flanagan)

The give-and-take is ideal, so that if you go down a second, all you have to do is to keep quiet and let someone else play for a second. In that way, the music continues to grow. (Lee Konitz)

These references to conversation, communication, negotiation, and creating conjure notions of partners working together instinctively to produce a whole that is greater than the sum of its parts. It implies a process of letting go of the self to join into relationships that are bigger than the individuals involved. It suggests aligning the actors so that their solutions accomplish more than any of the individuals could have managed on their own. If it can be shown that this alignment produces better outcomes for groups, teams, and organizations, then it should follow that a primary function in leadership is to inspire and organize groups in such a way that they can frequently achieve that coherence.

I have heard the same descriptions applied to sports teams as well. Soccer aficionados describe a beautiful interaction of players working together improvisationally to try to make something happen. It is on the one hand very egalitarian, with every player performing a function that is vital to the team's success, but also a process that lends itself to great virtuosity, in which individual capacity to perform at a level that involves both excellence and surprise also plays a critical role in the success of the team. A colleague of mine once described her passion for her own favorite sport of basketball in similar terms. An excellent team and excellent players learn together to understand and anticipate, not only one another but what the other team is doing as well, and so they cultivate a chemistry that can bring about unique and productive results. That chemistry reflects groups of individuals working together in a harmonious alignment, which is everyone's goal in a contemporary organization.

Looking More Closely for Order

This mirrors the complexity of chaos theory that began to unite scientists and mathematicians across a wide variety of disciplines in the last third of the twentieth century. What began to emerge over so many branches of learning is a realization that the world may tend toward chaos, but there is an order to that disarray, or a "fine structure hidden within a disorderly stream of data" (Gleik, 1987, p. 29). This presses us to look more closely at how groups of people are inter-acting, and to look more closely for order or alignment where none has otherwise been suspected or perceived.

The alignment in a group often goes unnoticed by those who are involved in it. I remember a follow-up visit I made to a negotiation session between teachers and managers I had helped to develop collaborative bargaining strategies. We agreed that we would begin the day with my observing how they were working together, so they resumed negotiations on an issue they had already started to address. After about a half hour, I began to feel a little impatient with the dis-cussions, so I interrupted and mentioned that I thought they were pretty much in agreement. "Oh no," they replied. "We're nowhere near finished with this issue." I asked them to let me test that assump-tion, and named the consensus I was hearing. To their surprise, everyone in the room indicated assent, and so they were able to move on in the agenda. The degree of coherence can be noticed in a group if the eye and the ear are trained to detect it in much the same way that a person can learn to discriminate the qualities and characteris-tics of a particular style of music or a sport.

A Science As Well As an Art

Scientific literature is filled with fascinating examples of research into this principle of alignment, and technology is delivering meth-ods of demonstrating the notion that it is possible to align people in ways that truly allow them to think together. However skeptically we might react to this notion, it does provide a concrete model of how the consciousness of two or more individuals can produce an align-ment that is deeper than normal experience has previously consid-ered possible. A series of physics experiments proposed by John Bell in the 1960s are frequently referenced as evidence of the intercon-nectedness in the natural world. Stated simply, they show that two microscopic particles have correlations that cannot be explained even when removed from each other by a large enough distance that they are not normally able to communicate with one another. So measurements to one of the objects will determine the outcome of measurements to the other (Goswami, 2000). While most physicists would be reluctant to relate the behavior of particles to people, it does at least provide a metaphor for describing one way to think about human consciousness.

When Life Imitates Physics

Jacobo Grinberg-Zylberbaum conducted research indicating that there is a similar correlation created when human subjects meditate together with the intent to establish a connection. When the subjects were separated afterward into isolated chambers and one of the two individuals was exposed to a light stimulus, the EEG of the second subject responded as if also exposed to the same stimulus (Laszlo, 1996). Physicists refer to this alignment as coherence, and it can be distinguished from incoherence by a dance analogy. A line of professional dancers all doing the same steps in unison, like the Radio City Rockettes or those in *Riverdance*, describes *phase coherence*. A group of random patrons in a nightclub, all dancing together on the same dance floor, but each improvising their own steps to the same rock music and behaving independently from one another, describes *phase incoherence* (Goswami, 2000, p. 68).

There are other examples from scientific literature suggesting the existence of a coherence principle that can align individuals. In a double-blind experiment, Krippner established the possibility that a "sender" concentrating on a randomly selected art print can influence the dreams of a subject. The study showed a significant correlation between the art print that was being "transmitted" and "considerably higher" scores on those evenings on which there was less geothermal activity impacting the area where the research was conducted (Persinger and Krippner, 1989). There are many other reports of "extranormal" connections analogous to the Bell experiments, between mothers and their children, between lovers, and between identical twins in which one individual reacts to a traumatic event experienced by the other though separated by large distances (Laszlo, 1996).

Evidence of Powerful Human Connections

There is also evidence that human consciousness can impact the natural world. Physicist Werner Heisenberg (1958) reasoned that the "reality" of an "event" is dependent on the nature of our "observation" of that event (p. 52). Researchers have also found that the behavior of random number generators becomes "positively non-random" at moments in modern history when the collective consciousness of a large number of people is focused on a single event, such as an important athletic event or the O.J. Simpson trial (Goswami, 2000). These experiments have been replicated at the Global Consciousness Project at Princeton University where they are collecting a database that includes a nonrandom curve lasting for two days after the events of September 11, 2001. While the GCP admits to little understanding of why it happens, they report on their observations as follows:

> While there are viable alternative explanations, the anomalous correlation is not a mistake or a misreading. It can be interpreted as a clear, if indirect, confirmation of the hypothesis that the (instruments') behavior is affected by global events and our reactions to them. This is startling in scientific terms because we do not have widely accepted models that accommodate such an interpretation of the data. More important than the scientific interpretation, however, may be the question of meaning. What shall we learn, and what should we do in the face of evidence that we may be part of a global consciousness? Of course, this is not a new idea or a novel question. The results from this scientific study are an apparent manifestation of the ancient idea that we are all interconnected, and that what we think and feel has effects on others, everywhere in the world. (Nelson, 2002, p. 567)

This research suggests the possibility that individuals in the world do have a measurable interconnection with one another when consciousness is collectively focused on or by a single event.

Similarly, Rupert Sheldrake (1999) reviews a large database giving evidence that dogs, cats, and other animals are connected to people, or to other animals, in ways that go beyond familiar sensory explanations. A typical account describes a story of an animal that can reliably predict the erratic behavior of the human master. Sheldrake describes "morphic fields" at work that are essentially identical to the behavior of the particles in Bell's experiments described above.

> Morphic fields link together the members of a social group . . . .
> A member who goes to a distant place still remains connected

to the rest of the group through this social field, which is elastic. Morphic fields would permit a range of telepathic influences to pass from animal to animal within a social group, or from person to person, or from person to companion animal. The ability of these fields to stretch out like invisible elastic bands enables them to act as channels for telepathic communication even over great distances (pp. 25–26).

I had an unsettling experience of my own a number of years ago that caused me to puzzle over how humans can connect. I was standing in my kitchen talking with my oldest daughter who was then in middle school. She was involved in a school project on spelling, and our discussion about her work triggered a memory from my seventh grade year about an old friend of mine—the best speller in the class—who made it to the finals of the regional spelling championship. As I was telling my daughter how we would tease him for weeks afterwards about the word he had missed, the telephone rang. "Hi, John; this is Bill" (my long lost friend).

I hadn't spoken to him for at least 20 years, and I was dumbfounded by the experience. There was a plausible reason for the call at that general period of time (he found my name in a high school reunion book that had only been published six months before) but it still seemed unfathomable that he would choose that five-minute window as the moment to place the transcontinental call. When I told him about his timing, he just laughed and said, "People tell me I have a knack for things like that." While I didn't fully appreciate it then, I have since realized that what happened that day was not only the result of some uncanny power of Bill's (for such experiences were beyond the norm for me), but also might be related to an unexplainable connection that was somehow linking us over the span of all that time and distance.

COHERENCE AND CONSCIOUSNESS

The theologian Teilhard de Chardin (1955) described the possibility of a consciousness connecting everyone in the world:

Everyone wants something larger, finer, better for mankind. Scattered throughout the apparently hostile masses which are fighting each other, there are elements everywhere which are only waiting for a shock in order to re-orientate themselves and unite. All that is needed is that the right ray of light should fall upon these men as upon a cloud of particles, that an appeal should be sounded which responds to their internal needs and across all denominations, across all the conventional barriers which still exist, we shall see the living atoms of the universe seek each other out, find each other and organize themselves (p. 33).

If we can accept the possibility of such a unifying principle, then in its simplest form it can transform the way we approach conflict. We can find ways of aligning, or realigning, the thinking of parties to disputes so that they are, in fact, "organizing themselves" in such a way that they are thinking together, rather than striving to impose a preferred point of view on the other. David Bohm (1980, 1990) was fascinated enough by the prospect of a coherence principle operating between human beings ("consciousness") that is similar to the correlation of particles ("matter") that he devoted much of his final years exploring interconnections between people through the process of dialogue (Bohm, 1980, p. 196).

Coherence and Organizational Leadership

My own professional practice over the past 30 years has led me to conclude intuitively what this emerging body of literature is beginning to document—that effective communications, problem solving, and conflict resolution in groups is, to a large measure, dependent on the degree of alignment that is created among the members of a given problem solving community. This possibility of a collective pool of consciousness that is greater than what is available to any of us as individuals certainly raises questions that defy our conventional understanding of the world. While there are no clear explanations yet for why or how this happens, there is increasing interest in the notion across a wide variety of disciplines. It is a major purpose of this book to understand coherence well enough to apply the principles to organizational leadership. This book will offer practitioners an approach to leadership that capitalizes on how people align to solve problems using the principles of coherence to ensure that the members of an organization are well situated to elegantly address the needs of the group and its members.

A Different Kind of Magic

Contrary to what many people hope, a skilled facilitator waving a magic marking pen over the group does not create coherence. However, a good leader or facilitator can help to create the right conditions for alignment to happen. For example, in a traditional argument the intent is to persuade others to accept and adopt our own point of view. Conversely, alignment is achieved by a group of people who think, listen, and talk together in such a fashion that they are able to free themselves from their preconceived notions and begin to understand new possibilities. A positive coherence is the result of a thoughtful interchange of thinking and ideas in which everyone realizes that an optimal result will probably lead to everyone seeing the world differently.

For example, I worked with a very divided city council in which the actions of individual members and their collective differences had caused the city manager to resign. They came to our first session filled with anger and blame directed at each other and at the departed chief executive. But as they began to talk together, they agreed that they shared a common goal, of attracting and retaining a new manager who would be able to lead them, and the city, more effectively. They acknowledged that their current dysfunctional rancor would discourage high caliber candidates from even applying to the position they desperately needed to fill. Their collective goal was bigger than their individual differences, so they began to open themselves up enough to discuss the assumptions about roles and behaviors that were resulting in the negativity and destructiveness. Once they moved past the accusations to allow for an open and honest reflection on their own problematic actions, they became aligned in a way that helped them move forward productively for their own governance team, as well as for the benefit of the city they were each obliged to serve.

Seeking a New Way of Doing Business

If the evolutionary notion of conflict is a signal to the body that it is time to generate the hormones that lead to fight-or-flight, the twenty-first century version is a signal from the organization or the relationship that there are problems needing attention. When I have had the opportunity to work with schools that are formally considered to be underperforming either by the faculty itself, the district, or the state, I have often found that the faculty was experiencing a level of interpersonal conflict that they felt was impeding their ability to successfully address issues related to student performance. In one case, the toxic interpersonal interactions of members of the faculty in general, and the leadership team in particular, included personal attacks and bitter interactions that left the staff members feeling divided and isolated. The resolution for them involved naming the competitive, adversarial behaviors and developing new habits designed to resolve divisive issues, rather than fighting over or avoiding them.

Conflict Resolution Begins With the Self

The solution begins with the self. Anyone who aspires to leadership must look inward with an eye and ear open to the probability that changing the world will start by changing oneself through a fundamental commitment to inquire and to learn. The most important skill that was cultivated on that school leadership team was the courage to name the attacking behaviors. The team members needed to recognize that they had been incapacitated by their own fight-or-flight responses, which in this case either meant standing by silently and fearfully, or engaging in verbal attacks out of habit and frustration. They eventually learned to look inward first to address the fears and the attitudes that were programming their habitual conflict.

Once they began to describe the behaviors without accusation or assumptions about intent, they began to realize that they were interacting with each other more respectfully and productively. It is futile to blame others in our interpersonal or organizational conflicts because in a conflicted situation there is very little we can do to change other people, but a lot we can do to change ourselves. As we will explore further in Chapter 3, examining our own motives and interactions makes us much more able to impact others, and ultimately the world around us.

Collaborate Because It Delivers Better Results

Most of us probably cultivate a set of problem-solving strategies for very pragmatic and practical reasons. When there is conflict that is keeping us from getting important work done, we strive to resolve it so that we can get on with our business. I experienced this very reasonable strategy almost two decades ago when I worked with colleagues to repair an educational labor relationship that had become so dysfunctional that it was impeding the ability of educators to work together to support student learning. In fact, we used the dysfunction as a rationale to sell our constituencies on the idea of cooperating with one another, rather than fighting. We pointed out to them that we could get settlements just as beneficial as had been produced adversarially, and with much less disruption.

As we began to move forward collaboratively, we realized that a greater purpose was being served with the potential to provide our organization and its members with bigger payoffs if we could align ourselves as partners around our collective tasks, such as improving employee performance or wrestling with budget deficits. More important, we have gradually been discovering that the business of educating students in an increasingly high-stakes environment for the neediest of learners is so difficult and complex that it requires faculty to be able to collaborate together to improve teaching and learning throughout the organization. I see this same hunger in many other organizations whose adversarial rancor and discord impede the ability to pass ballot measures and bond issues and to effectively deliver core services. As alignment occurs, leaders begin to pick up the phone and call each other before small organizational rubs become huge conflicts. More important, key actors already know what to do, because they have had deep conversations about what is important, and they have empowered one another to act on behalf of those core needs.

SUMMARY

Public sector organizations in today's complex environment require high levels of collaboration, communication, and problem solving to meet the high expectations of the society they serve. This means that the people in those organizations must manage habitual fight-or-flight responses to conflict in order to find ways of interacting that promote more creative and broadly beneficial outcomes. Leaders responsible for producing these outcomes can utilize natural principles of alignment to develop a level of communication and interaction that many people never suspect is possible.

Cultivating an ability to detect coherence (or incoherence) and to promote the attitudes and skills that help create it should not only produce better outcomes for the organization and its stakeholders, but it should also support a stronger community and more fulfilling lives for the individual members. But the ability to lead groups to greater alignment and more effective agreements begins with the self, and the ability of each prospective leader to understand how his or her own behaviors can promote conflict or alignment in the broader group. Chapter 2 will consider how an individual leader can cultivate habits designed to promote more effective agreements in groups.

CHAPTER TWO

Starting With the Self

*Attitudes and Habits
That Promote Collaboration*

T he principle of coherence is a focus in this book for the "magic" that can be unleashed when it is applied to conflict resolution. Leaders who are open to seeing the world differently create the conditions that support bona fide learning. As discussed in the last chapter, individuals can also learn to create together in a way that allows them to override their traditional fight-or-flight responses to problems and to produce surprisingly elegant and successful results. This requires a willingness to exchange control for discovery, and to embrace the chaos of conflict for all it can teach us about how the natural world harmoniously self-organizes. An effective problem solver welcomes and values the discomfort that comes with giving up favorite ways of seeing the world in order to create new and more productive perspectives.

Several years ago I worked with a group of managers and labor representatives from four contiguous cities. They had been talking together for several years about the possibility of coordinating and sharing a variety of fire protection services. They recognized that a great deal of money might be saved while providing much more efficient and effective fire protection services for the citizens of all four cities if they could eliminate duplication and redundancy by sharing services that each were separately offering. For example, each of the four cities had a battalion chief on duty at all times to oversee the activities of the fire companies, when two or three could amply have covered all four cities. The savings could be used for more effective department operations, to upgrade equipment, and to raise salaries.

Most stakeholders saw great potential for the reorganization, but there were many competing dynamics at work that were contributing to discord and breakdown. Some firefighters wanted a promise that salaries among the departments would immediately be aligned with the highest paying city. Others wanted to be sure that the restructuring would not compromise their desire for promotional opportunities. The middle managers responsible for implementing the shared services needed to know that any new system would be a manageable one before they could commit to it. The city managers wanted assurance that any restructuring would cost no more money during tough financial times in which all of them were struggling to make cuts in their overall city budgets. There was a complex system at work, and many of these motives appeared to be contradictory, to the extent that implementing one would seem to deny another.

Negotiating all these perspectives with at least four different levels in each of the four different organizations promised to be an adversarial fiasco. But they also knew that to be successful, they needed to regroup in a way that kept them as much as possible on one team versus the 16 different stakeholder groups that came to the table.

A JOURNEY OF DISCOVERY, NOT A FORMULA

Many leaders who organize and facilitate meetings strive to move the group efficiently through the problem solving process, with each step of the agenda carefully crafted to produce a desired outcome. While I certainly aspire to such "tidy" meetings myself, often it becomes clear, even after a thorough premeeting assessment, that until we have told the story together and had an opportunity to understand the dynamics that the diverse individuals bring into the room, we can only guess about what we will need to do by the end of the meeting. We could organize the first two to three hours of the meeting with a tight agenda, but until everyone better understood the patterns and dynamics that defined how this group would come together, it was pure speculation where the meeting would need to go next. This illustrates an important principle related to aligning people in groups through problem solving: It's a *heuristic*, not an *algorithm*, or that which is learned through discovery, rather than a logical sequence of steps. I use these "overbearing" terms because, when they have been defined in the context of problem solving, they help shape an attitude that is critical to leading groups effectively.

Looking for the Recipe

Problem solving and conflict resolution workshops are popular these days, filled with participants eager to discover the recipe or formula that holds the key to success. Our attraction to order prompts us to look for a logical progression of steps that will lead us successfully through a task at hand. Certainly cooking is that way, and numerous other concrete activities like planting a garden, setting up a new appliance, or assembling prefabricated bookshelves. Any of these tasks can, to some extent, be set down in a progression of actions that if followed in the prescribed order will generally lead to a successful conclusion.

But this natural fondness for a recipe or *algorithm* (the logical step-by-step procedure for solving a mathematical problem) is often frustrated when we discover that conflict is rarely so orderly or predictable that it lends itself to a formulaic approach. When I cook something for the first time, I generally follow a recipe because of the likelihood that it will produce a known commodity, especially because I am a far cry from being a master chef. The result is usually one that I have conceived in advance, based on the promise of the picture in the book or magazine, or my own notion of how the dish should look, smell, and taste.

My life as a public school administrator is a whole lot less predictable than my life in the kitchen. There are few recipes available to lead me to my desired outcome as I struggle to cope with the realities, the possibilities, and the surprises that continually confront a school district leader. While there are some tools and approaches that will be useful in many different situations, it is essential to recognize that problems are a bit like snowflakes—no two are alike, and so with each new situation learning will be the order of the day.

Expecting the Unexpected

Effective problem solving leads to discovery rather than to a preconceived outcome. A skillful leader enters the process expecting to be surprised by the result, and thus is focused on learning, with the assumption that the process will lead to seeing the world differently. Problem solving presents a means of inquiring into the nature of a situation, to notice patterns and to strive to form elegant solutions that will bring seemingly conflicting perspectives into harmony, or coherence. This provides a framework of attitudes as well as skills that makes it easier for traditional adversaries to work together on one page, and to create outcomes that are consistent with the needs of each.

In this approach, effective problem solving is a *heuristic* (a process that leads to learning or discovery), and so it reflects an attitude, not an algorithm. When we attempt to resolve a thorny problem, it is difficult to control how the issue unfolds. A skillful problem solver understands that a successful session often ends with everyone seeing the world differently than they did before they started. This involves expecting the unexpected and requires the skills and tools to respond accordingly.

I worked with an advocate on a complex planning issue who was so preoccupied with the form of the agenda for each meeting that he became very distracted when forces beyond his control caused those agendas to change. He would become so undone by any bump or pothole along his expected path that he was less effective as an advocate for his client. So much of his attention and his energy were focused on a futile effort to manage the process in a way that would produce his preferred outcome, that he easily came unglued by surprises and responded with anger and hostility that undermined the relationships he so badly needed in order to complete the project successfully. More specifically, his inflexibility left him unable to learn from, and respond to, unexpected opposition to the project, and he remained rigidly attached to his own perspective. The result was costly delays in the planning process, and eventually a denial of his project by the city council.

A great problem solver is comfortable with the uncertainty of not knowing the right answer, and will have at his or her disposal the skills and tools necessary to navigate the way from uncertainty to an acceptable outcome. A number of those practical tools and skills that are intended to help cultivate effective problem solving are presented in Part II of this book. They are not offered as a formula for how to get from point A to point B, but rather as resources to support attitudes of openness, learning, and discovery that are essential to effective conflict resolution in complex systems.

The cities negotiating the shared fire services had been talking for several years without being able to get themselves aligned enough to move forward. Their success involved acknowledging relatively early on that it would be impossible to give everyone what they wanted *immediately*, but that a shared effort had the promise of *eventually* meeting everyone's needs sufficiently. After a couple of hours of discussion with this new mindset they realized that they were sidestepping the hard issues, and so focused their discussions around the areas of greatest vulnerability.

By the time that day concluded, many misconceptions had been clarified, including the notion that all four cities needed to participate for the project to move forward, and what might logically happen if any stakeholders chose not to take part. The day ended with some honest conversation, and with many of the participants feeling uncomfortable and agitated by the choices that had been outlined. Despite their discomfort, most participants checked out of that meeting indicating they had accomplished much more than they had hoped would be possible, and that going to that place of deep uncertainty made it possible for them to understand the choices clearly enough to prepare for the decision point that was so badly needed. It was only after they let go of their need to control the outcomes that they became open to the unexpected possibilities that offered a truly acceptable resolution, which came in the form of much more complex combinations of shared services and consolidations than anyone had imagined possible when they started.

MAINTAINING AN ATTITUDE OF OPENNESS

So problem solving leads to a sense of discovery, and an effective problem solver must be open to the possibility of learning something new, however unsettling the discovery might prove to be. Often leaders are perceived by their colleagues as not wanting to know what they might be doing wrong. One school superintendent was seen by subordinates as only wanting to hear "the good stuff" and easy to anger when presented with negative feedback. As a result, they were far less likely to give her information that seemed critical in nature. Whether or not their perception of her was true, that leader was not only alienating her team, but worse, she was not

Table 2.1   Attitudes and Behaviors During Conflict

Open	Closed
Open minds	Hidden agendas
Respect for the other position	Emotions
Defining problem up front	"Me only"
Cooperation	Assumptions
Commitment to a solution	Fixed conclusions
Willingness to meet others' needs	Positionalism
Compromise	Personal attacks
"Win-win" possibility	Lack of communication
Commitment to excellence	Lack of information
Objective	Lack of listening
Better rapport	Misstating facts
No personalization	Personality conflict
Lots of listening and communication,	Defensiveness
plenty of information	Old history comes into play

getting access to the thinking that might have helped her to improve her leadership.

By contrast, another school superintendent who eagerly pressed for any insight into how his own behavior might be contributing to a breakdown with the teachers union was able to notice a pattern of well-intentioned actions that were causing the union leadership to perceive paternalistic treatment, rather than the partnership the superintendent was trying to create. By being open to potentially negative information, he was able to adjust his own behavior in a way that caused the union leadership to change as well.

I often illustrate this principle with workshop participants by asking them to describe the qualities, characteristics, and behaviors when problem solving breaks down. The results developed by one group are listed in the right-hand column of Table 2.1.

Similarly, the left-hand column of Table 2.1 was created when the same participants were asked to describe what it looks like when conflict situations are successfully resolved. This group was typical of most, creating a list of qualities that were characteristically *open* or vulnerable to describe what they expected would work and listing *closed* or defensive qualities to describe what does not work, and so we label the columns accordingly in Table 2.1.

MOVING TOWARD GREATER MINDFULNESS

Uninitiated workshop participants consistently recreate Table 2.1, which suggests that there is an experience base and an inner wisdom that allows most people to be able to identify the open behaviors that will lead to success in problem solving, and the closed behaviors that tend to lead to adversarialism. Why then is there so much closed behavior in conflict situations and why is there so much unresolved conflict? Part of the answer can be found in the discussion in Chapter 1 on how the human organism responds to the stressors that come with conflict. The characteristics of the right-hand column in Table 2.1 correspond to the symptoms of fight and flight, and as already discussed, we are genetically wired so those responses kick in more rapidly than our more rational thinking processes, infusing the relationship with defensive "us versus them" attitudes and behaviors that undermine problem solving. I see these tendencies in my own school district, in which we need to be extremely mindful to ensure that we are not pitting schools against each other in competition for staff, scarce financial resources, or the best way to approach student achievement. Fullan (2003) reiterates the need for open behavior by suggesting that the real business of school reform is so complex and behavior so entrenched that long-lasting reform will only be possible when it is implemented collaboratively, not only by teachers within school teams, but more important, across district and regional lines.

Closed behaviors also inhibit learning by restricting the flow of information, and thus promote free agency rather than collaboration. A different set of habits is needed to enable these independent actors to begin working effectively together. We must be aware of our tendency to defect and instead maintain attitudes as well as skills that allow us to mindfully practice the qualities of openness that are described in the left-hand side of Table 2.1.

The Effect of Habit on Our Ability to Stay Open

This tendency toward defensive or competitive actions, despite our best intentions, has been characterized by Argyris (1993) as "Model I" behavior. He points out that our habitual actions, and the systems we create around us, inhibit our learning when they cause us to behave in ways that are closed and self-protective. Argyris (1993, 2000) describes "organizational defensive routines" that isolate leaders from the data, information, and input that might enable them to avert the kinds of problems that ultimately result in uncontrolled conflict.

That superintendent whose subordinates are convinced that she is unable or unwilling to hear criticism is setting herself up for a string of avoidable organizational troubles, because whether intentionally or not, she has been "closed" off from the kinds of input and interactions that can guarantee her learning in the organization. Argyris and Schon (1974) dubbed this behavior in which leaders operate from the closed perspective as "mystery and mastery." Practitioners operating in this mode attempt to gain tactical advantage by controlling information. Unfortunately, when information is not readily available, collaboration with the rest of the organization is discouraged and alignment can only occur based on what the leader chooses to share.

> *For an excellent analysis of how to adopt the concepts of openness and learning to coaching, see* Masterful Coaching *by Robert Hargrove.*

The right-hand column of Table 2.2 describes the operating values that are in place when a leader engages in Model I or closed behavior. It has been adopted from Argyris (1993), Hargrove (1995), and Glaser (2001).

As we will discuss in greater detail in Chapter 3, the values described in the Model I column of Table 2.2 occur very naturally in the form of competitive and self-protective actions that we exhibit, even when that adversarialism goes against our own interests.

These habits are evident one-on-one, as in the case of the teacher who takes a very self-protective stance when faced with a parent who comes in to complain about a student's grade. The behaviors can also appear organizationally, as in the rancorous relationship between one large school district and its teachers union, which endured a strike together every time the collective bargaining agreement needed to be renegotiated. Even though all the key leaders at the bargaining table wanted to change those habits, the union constituents had been "trained" over many years that the best deal did not come until power and leverage were asserted, and so they found themselves pulled back to an adversarial place by a constituency and a couple of key leaders who seemed wired to respond that way.

Society Loves a Good Fight

Outside influences can also impact the ability of public relationships to stay open. Deborah Tannen (1998) describes how the

Table 2.2   Operating Values

Model II (Open)	Model I (Closed)
1. Relatedness—create shared meaning	1. Separateness—achieve my own intended purpose
2. Maximize effectiveness by searching for the best approach	2. Maximize winning by trying to impose my will
3. Vigilant monitoring to detect and correct errors and deficiencies	3. Suppress negative feelings and avoid vulnerability
4. Maintain and inspire joint commitment to the endeavor	4. Seek unilateral control of self and others
5. Learning—being good allows me to look good	5. Performing—avoid looking bad

media and our popular culture pit us against each other, even when we are inclined to cooperate. I experienced this firsthand while helping a city and a developer to engage with citizens in a neighborhood where the city was planning to build an affordable housing project.

The city manager envisioned a collaborative process in which the city would work proactively with the neighbors in order to avoid the "not in my back yard" (NIMBY) syndrome that is so prevalent in endeavors of this nature. The first meeting began a bit acrimoniously, as might have been predicted, as concerns and anxieties were shared. But that was the purpose of the meeting, and eventually we began to chart a list of the interests that neighbors brought to the process and some ideas they had for how the plan could be improved. While we were still far from an agreement when the meeting ended, the neighbors, although still suspicious and somewhat untrusting, had begun to align with the city and the developer around the possibility that the development could be designed in a way that addressed their needs acceptably. Although no one realized it at the time, a neighbor suggested a breakthrough option that night that ended up resolving many of the most vocal concerns. The meeting adjourned amicably two and a half hours later with some tangible sense of hopefulness for the future.

The reporter who covered the meeting reported on the disagreements that he thought were most newsworthy, and the copy editor picked up on those differences with a headline proclaiming "NIMBY-ism Strikes . . . Complaints abound about plan for 120 units of affordable housing." Whether or not we feel we can influence the way our business is reported by the media, it is important to understand that adversarial behavior is often considered to be more newsworthy than collaboration. Somehow we have programmed our culture to accentuate the fight. How refreshing it would have been to read a headline proclaiming: "Thoughtful Discussions and Ideas Frame Local Conversations about Affordable Housing." Actually, the newspaper may have helped push us closer to the coherence the city manager had envisioned by angering the neighbors enough with the "NIMBYism" charge for them to embrace the right plan.

See Chapter 3, page 36 for an example of an instance in which the press did report on thoughtful problem solving.

Staying Open When We Really Want to Be Closed

A closer look at the left-hand column of Table 2.2 reveals a set of values that describe how to maintain openness. The trouble is, when we most need to stay open, we are most likely to be closed and self-protective. When we are feeling the most threatened and at risk is also the time that we most need to maximize our learning by being open and vulnerable, and that goes against everything that we have practiced over a lifetime of fight-or-flight responses. This means that we need to cultivate habits that enable us to stay in the conversation when we are most inclined to hunker down self-protectively. If we do not create opportunities for deep conversations with those we perceive to be most opposed to us, we almost guarantee that we will fail to achieve an agreement on anything. Our tendency to return to the habitual fear-based responses built into our central nervous systems as the first line reaction to stress often leads to disastrous consequences. New approaches are needed as we attempt to improve our ability to coexist within relationships, families, organizations, and local or international communities without resorting to battle.

Maintaining Mindfulness

There is a long tradition in individual and organizational learning that aspires to achieve a Zen-like state in which the practitioner can perform a skill without thinking about it. Two classical examples are tying a bowknot or riding a bike. Once I know how to do it, I don't need to think about it. Similarly, outstanding athletes whose swings or shots are perfectly "grooved" have nothing to keep them from being in the moment of the game. On the other hand, when I have just learned a skill I think awkwardly and self-consciously about each of the elements of the task I'm performing.

When it comes to conflict and communication, individuals must maintain the same mindful approach as a novice—that is, ever aware of what they are thinking and doing. As soon as we allow unconscious routines to take over this function, we run the risk of the old fight-or-flight habits kicking in. This involves a focus that is in many ways unique to modern human experience. LeDoux (1996) is optimistic about our ability to evolve as a species in a way that brings about "a more harmonious integration of reason and passion" (p. 303). But until evolution rewires those emotional responses, a different level of attention is required if we are to avoid disastrous adversarial conflicts, whether in the workplace, the home, the freeway, or the world's geopolitical stage.

SUMMARY

Leaders and groups who can cultivate the ability to stay open and vulnerable when they are most inclined to feel defensive and self-protective will be well poised to problem solve effectively. A willingness to confront the blunt realities that honest information provides us when we have a problem gives access to solutions that are not available to those who remain closed. That same openness allows us to let go of our preconceived notions of how an issue ought to be resolved, and to prepare to be delightfully surprised when unexpected solutions are allowed to surface.

A leader becomes a powerful problem solver by modeling that openness on a very personal level and by remaining mindfully aware of the habits that lead to learning and discovery. This makes it possible to create communities of learners who practice those habits collaboratively to create dynamic work teams who can efficiently solve problems and create shared meaning as they strive to focus together to push the business of their organizations to more effective levels. The next chapter describes those behaviors that lie at the heart of effective collaborative teams.

CHAPTER THREE

Creating Shared Meaning

Moving From Discord to Collaboration

W e have been exploring how effective problem solving involves an open attitude that enables the key players to access information that will lead to learning and discovery. So how does an individual leader who is personally primed for openness and inquiry positively influence a group that seems otherwise inclined? In this chapter we will explore the attitudes and general approaches that can allow a leader to find common ground and produce shared meaning even in situations in which the participants are experiencing a significant amount of conflict.

ALIGNING THE TEAM

The closed and competitive attitudes many people habitually bring to workplace interactions cause them to see others as their adversaries. I have often heard comments from teachers about how aggressive parents can be when they come to talk about students. Staff members characterize overbearing parents as a divisive factor in the school because they are willing and eager to pit one teacher against another in their efforts to further their children's academic careers. Similarly, parents often characterize the school conference room as a hostile and intimidating place with mysterious and confusing rules and terminology that has them feeling as if the deck has been stacked against them by uncaring professionals with ulterior motives. In other schools, parent seems to be pitted against parent and teacher against teacher in the daily struggle for survival in what feels like an increasingly high-stakes world.

A Tendency Toward "Us" Against "Them"

This "us against them" dynamic is typical in many workplace and customer service interactions, and so a leader who is trying to nurture an environment characterized by honest, respectful, and productive conversations that are focused on a common vision must find a way to bring an end to the fight-or-flight behaviors that promote adversarialism.

It is difficult getting people into the same room together to talk about dicey or difficult subjects. Often there are taboo topics that people avoid at all costs because they are uncomfortable, despite the potential for making things better if resolved. I worked with a school district that had experienced a very bitter and divisive strike a number of years before, and we discovered that many of the managers and board members still had some festering feelings about the strike and its impact.

It can also be very intimidating to think about having a conversation about a topic about which one feels emotionally vulnerable. Even when the right people are assembled in a room together to address an uncomfortable topic, we try to protect ourselves with closed and defensive habits, which often have us poised for a competitive battle as we prepare to reflect or to negotiate. Those people who engage with us pick up on that defensiveness and, as a result, everyone hunkers down for a confrontation. An effective leader needs to be thinking about how to break down the defensiveness.

Typically, when we sit down to address a problem we even tend to organize ourselves in a fashion that promotes adversarial behavior. This competitive configuration is depicted in Figure 3.1.

We sit across the table from each other just as the teams in a football or soccer game or the contestants in a wrestling match might be positioned at the opening whistle. We set ourselves up with the X's squared off against the O's, so that the focus is literally on the people, rather than the problem. Anyone who has participated in a traditional collective bargaining process will recognize the "playing field" and can relate to the spirit of competition that it promotes. The field that encompasses "the team" clearly separates the X's from the

Figure 3.1   Attacking the People

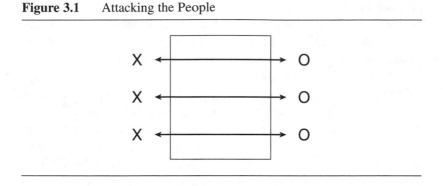

O's in a way that encourages a mindset that has each focused on addressing its own needs, if necessary at the expense of the other.

Drawing a Circle Around the Whole Group

This is not to say that collaboration is impossible in an "X versus O" configuration, for savvy problem solvers can deliver elegant results in any arrangement. But the potential for bringing a group to agreement can be significantly increased by mindfully organizing participants in advance so that the appropriate parties to a decision are physically in the room in the first place and a figurative circle of inclusion is drawn around all the key stakeholders. Figure 3.2 illustrates how this might look. The group has been configured with the X's and the O's intermixed. Everyone can see one

Figure 3.2   Attacking the Problem

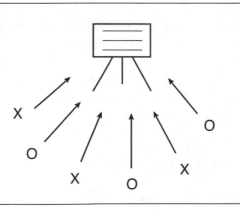

another and they are facing the chart, board, or projection screen that captures the critical elements of the problem solving process. There are no real or artificial barriers separating the individuals or the groups, and they keep the problem as their mutual focus.

We have discovered over the years that it can be extremely helpful to force participants out of their customary comfort zones in order to help them to see everyone in the group as a potential ally. This can be as easy as asking staff participants to mix themselves around the room to ensure that "customers" have places to intermingle, or including a ground rule that requires mixed seating. Many collective bargaining teams have a ground rule stipulating that while the two teams are together in problem solving negotiations, they will mix their seating according to Figure 3.2 to ensure a sense of "us," rather than "we versus they."

> *For more information on dialogue and how to facilitate it, see William Isaacs, Linda Ellinor and Glenna Gerard, and Daniel Yankelovich. All are listed in the References.*

Sometimes situations call for the group to sit in a full circle, again with the "X and O" participants well mixed, as shown in Figure 3.3. This format might be used in formal dialogue as a way of deeply listening to one another and slowing down the conversation. The circle creates a sense of enclosure that allows eye contact and makes it easy for participants to "speak to the center" of the group, rather than addressing individuals. Care should be taken to ensure that latecomers or introverts are included in the circle and not allowed to sit in a way that isolates them from the group. What is most important is that thought is given to how the actual physical organization of participants can be managed to ensure that the process supports the desired outcome; that everyone in the room understands that they are on the same team; and that they interact accordingly.

It is also critical to work to ensure that everyone is aligned around the problem. Chapter 6 will focus on how to define the problem or the task in a way that ensures that problem solving begins with participants all on the same page.

CHANGING THE MINDSET

It can certainly be a substantial accomplishment to get the appropriate parties to an issue into a room together and configured as a

Figure 3.3   Organizing for Dialogue

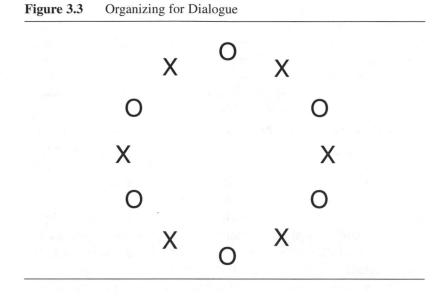

single team to begin problem solving. The next critical consideration is to create an atmosphere that gets everyone thinking and
acting as if they are working together on one team. So long
as people are wired for competition they will tend to compete.
Help participants to presume collaboration, and they will tend to
behave quite collaboratively. This rewiring can commence at the
beginning of the meeting when the leader names the vision of a
single team.

Creating the "Container" for Problem Solving

In Chapter 1, I mentioned a school group whose interactions
were characterized by bitter infighting. The first thing that was done
to reprogram that group was to develop ground rules that would
allow them to attack problems rather than each other. It actually took
a couple of hours and some intense negotiations before there was
enough trust for them to agree on some basic behavioral expectations even for that meeting, but by the time they were done, people
were working together in a way they had never thought possible.
Whether or not as a direct result of this aligning of behavior and
expectations, the school was honored a number of years later as a
high performing school.

It is often the case that simply setting clear and understandable expectations for how people will interact causes them to behave more appropriately toward each other. I facilitated a formal planning commission meeting, and when it was all over, the local press commended the planning director, city manager, and commission chair for bringing in a neutral facilitator to ensure that all the parties would communicate and problem solve respectfully. In fact, I added very little to the content of the discussion. My main function in that meeting was simply to create and preside over a space where people could come together to address problems effectively. That space "container" needed to include an interactive climate that ensured that the traditional, adversarial relationships that had stymied the project for a number of years were transformed in such a way that all participants could focus on the creation of a project that would acceptably address everyone's needs. It is amazing to realize that the careful creation of a problem solving "container" in a governmental meeting is so rare that it is newsworthy. But the fact that it was reported is also encouraging.

While the high-stakes nature of this meeting may have justified an outside facilitator, many internal leaders are able to nurture effective problem solving in their own environments by creating and enforcing behavioral expectations that promote that sense of team. In our school district we have tried to encourage all school and district level teams to create written expectations that draw the circle around all stakeholders so that they feel like they are part of the same team. While most site leaders are comfortable with this task, facilitation support is available from the district and union leadership if it is needed.

> *For more information on sample ground rules and how to create a container for problem solving see Chapter 6.*

STAYING ON THE SAME PAGE

A number of years ago when I was serving as an assistant superintendent of schools, a colleague and I were meeting with a group of principals in our district to discuss a concept we were developing with the teachers association. The idea was an unpopular one with the principals, and they were giving us quite an earful of objections they brought to the conversation. Eventually one of them said, "Okay, let's vote." My colleague and I quickly moved to avoid that outcome, which we felt would only polarize the association and the principals, and so we closed the discussion by saying "That won't be necessary. We have a pretty good idea of your concerns about this concept. Let us take them to the union, and we'll see if we can come back to you with a new version that better meets your needs."

About a week later one of the principals approached me in the hallway and asked for a moment of my time. "A few of us really resented the way you manipulated that meeting last week," she confided. Puzzled by the disclosure, but glad to have this honest window into her thinking, I asked her to tell me more. "Well, we tried to vote on that issue, and you wouldn't let us because you knew that you would lose!"

The information surprised me. My colleague and I had been doing our best to keep everyone on one page as we went between the two groups to try to build a consensus on the project we were developing. Once we better understood their needs, we knew we needed to get back to work with the union to improve it accordingly. The principals did not like the project as they saw it, and wanted to kill it outright. They brought a naturally democratic mindset to the meeting, as we had always encouraged them to do, and sensing that the majority did not like it, they wanted to close the topic with a vote, as if to say, "Okay, this idea is a loser, let's kill it and move on to something else." I appreciated the insight this principal offered, and realized how miserably I had failed to communicate our true intent in the meeting, which was to listen and to learn how the project could be improved, rather than trying to sell them a "done deal," or for that matter to get a finished package from the principals.

An Inquiry Approach to Problem Solving

This winner and loser outlook is a common one and is often unnecessary. When the forthright principal learned that our true intent was to continue inquiring into the problem with the union until we could bring back something that would meet everyone's needs acceptably, she agreed that it was a sensible way to proceed. But we tend to bring into problem solving our own, separate perspectives for what the solution should be as well as what the process should look like, and our natural inclination is to strive to impose it on others, as in a debate. Unfortunately, this tends to create an advocacy spiral as the parties argue more and more aggressively for their own point of view. The end result will lead either to a stalemate, which results in no action, or to someone giving in, creating a win/lose conclusion.

Our goal as we move toward coherence is to keep the parties working mutually on the same page as members of one team in pursuit of one solution that meets everyone's needs acceptably, rather than allowing them to polarize around conflicting views. In this context we carefully avoid clinging to separate positions in order to ensure that the search for solutions is a joint one designed to achieve the satisfaction of every stakeholder. Part II of this book will focus on specific behaviors that make it possible to avoid such polarization.

A Different Kind of Vision

Once we consciously draw our circle around everyone involved in our problem solving, we begin to realize that we need to think differently about the task at hand. I become a more effective problem solver when I start to worry about producing outcomes that are as acceptable to others as they are to me. This means bringing a different kind of vision to what I am trying to accomplish and it requires mindfulness at all times to ensure that I am acting in a way that is consistent with that vision. I have a colleague who is a city manager, who articulates how helpful this notion can be in working with the city council. He describes how important it is to reprogram the traditional council notion that it only takes three votes to get your way. He is continually asking the council, "Why settle for a 3 to 2 vote that leaves someone mad at you, when you can work a little bit harder to come up with a 5 to 0 vote that has everyone feeling satisfied?" The key is to frame a concept for an acceptable solution in a way that addresses the core needs of all the constituents and then to act in a manner that is consistent with that vision.

See Chapter 4, page 63 for an example of how and why this city manager implements this premise and Chapter 7 for more on how to keep a focus on the vision in problem solving and decision making.

Moving Toward Generative Engagement

Most organizations aspire to what I call *generative engagement*, a high performance, collaborative level of interaction and production. Groups in generative engagement are able to keep everyone working together as one team and to create consensus-based solutions to problems in a manner that accepts the validity of everyone's interests and that searches for solutions that effectively address each of those needs. They see each other as equals and as allies, and they approach their world with creativity, openness, and an optimistic orientation to the future.

Needless to say, not all groups have such an orientation. One of the enlightening benefits of work as an organizational consultant is the opportunity to help and at the same time to observe and learn from organizations that find themselves involved in a level of discord that has become distracting enough that it is negatively impacting the effectiveness of the group. At that point someone has said, "Wait a minute; there has to be a better way to do this." This is essentially a voice from the organization naming the incoherence and calling for more effective alignment.

Stages of Group Development

Figure 3.4 (expanded from Glaser, 2001, and originally adapted from C. Otto Scharmer in Issacs, 1999, and Scharmer, 2001) describes stages of group development in a way that allows us to understand how groups evolve and, more important, what we need to do in order to make it more likely that they will become creative and dynamic learning organizations with a high level of coherence. An understanding of this framework can be useful in considering the developmental needs of a personal relationship or a family, as well as a professional work group. This model has also been significantly influenced by Bruce Tuckman (1965) and Scott Peck (1987). Each of these models conceptualizes four stages of group development that describe how a collection of individuals evolves together to the highest performing place. Figure 3.5 compares the descriptive stage of each of those models. A collective consideration of these frameworks is particularly helpful in understanding how the natural dynamics of group development can be harnessed by a leader to move an organization to a higher performing place.

Figure 3.4   Moving Toward Generative Engagement

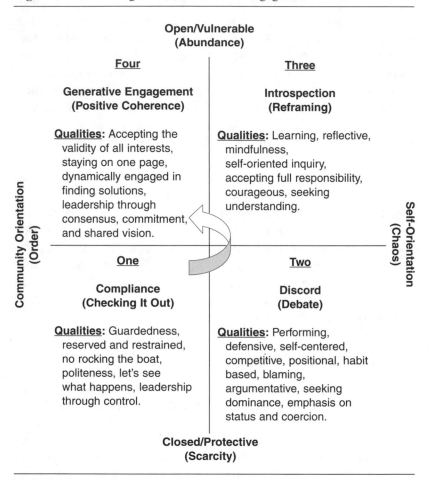

Figure 3.4 shows there are at least two critical dimensions that are influencing the evolution of a set of individuals on a team. The first is a tension between an orientation to the community and to the self. The second involves the dynamic already discussed in-depth between open and closed behaviors.

A Conflicted Governing Board

Perhaps the easiest way to understand the model is by applying it to a "real-life" example. A colleague of mine accepted a job offer as a superintendent of schools. His research and experience in the

Figure 3.5   Stages of Group Development—Comparison

Figure 3.4	Tuckman (1965)	Peck (1987)	Scharmer (2001)/ Issacs (1999)
Compliance	Forming	Pseudo Community	Politeness
Discord	Storming	Chaos	Breakdown
Introspection	Norming	Emptiness	Inquiry
Generative Engagement	Performing	Community	Flow

interviewing process made it clear to him that there were some significant problems among the board team, and so, as a condition of employment, he exacted a promise from the board to participate in a problem solving process that would result in clear expectations about how the board members as well as the new superintendent would all do business together. I was invited to provide support to that conversation.

His experiences in the interview and hiring process for the position, and my own premeeting assessment, uncovered some real animosity between individual board members that had a negative influence on the work of the board. The most offensive activities included what was perceived to be power plays over control of the agenda, public attacks, and other disrespectful behaviors. As is often the case on governing boards, some of the ill will had to do with political differences and some negativity carried over from the last election campaign. The board had set into a pattern of discord as characterized in quadrant two by closed and self-oriented behavior that was defensive and competitive based on the animosities that had developed. That included an assumption of scarcity, that is, that we cannot all have our way, so I need to work hard to ensure that my "way" prevails. So that was the problematic but not so unusual place they found themselves when their new chief executive joined the team and set out to provide leadership to take them to a different place. Figure 3.4 can help us to track their efforts to work effectively together from that point forward.

Quadrant One: Compliance—Don't Rock the Boat!

With the addition of a new superintendent that all board members supported, the negative behaviors had "gone underground." The board team moved comfortably back to "compliance," described as "everyone is on their best behavior." The focus is on the community, but there is a reserved and guarded quality to that orientation. Isaacs (1999, pp. 259–261) calls this stage "politeness," which aptly describes how people interact. As we will see in Chapter 4, there is coherence in this stage, but it has a negative quality to it. People are working together because they just do not want to make waves. While the board was in this stage in large measure because of the "honeymoon" relationship with the new CEO, many organizations operate indefinitely in "compliance" if there is a leadership structure that wants a high degree of order, and does not reward or honor risk taking. A totalitarian regime such as Saddam Hussein's tenure in Iraq typically operates indefinitely in this quadrant because people are too fearful to push against authority or each other. While many people function very happily in compliance—"just tell me what you want me to do"—it is not a place that lends itself to creative thinking and the generation of elegant solutions because people are so closed and self-protective that important ideas and information are guarded, rather than being readily available to the collaborative efforts of all group members.

Almost every workshop or retreat begins with compliance. Teachers recognize it every year when a new class filled with bright, shiny faces assembles for the first time. Almost every meeting begins in quadrant one as well, and it is an opportunity for whoever is in charge of the group's process to help establish a container that will lead to creative and productive outcomes. Similarly, that superintendent/board team was quickly able to agree on a set of ground rules that would promise to address the kinds of behavior that were considered the most disruptive.

This community orientation includes an attraction to order. Group members at least begin on their best behavior either out of inertia or guardedness. Even those who come with an ax to grind are usually waiting for the right moment to toss a stone of discord into the still pool of compliance that prevails at the start. That period of politeness was further exploited in the superintendent/board retreat by asking the participants to tell the stories that brought them together in that room that day to organize their work as a team. Connections were made between the people that opened everyone up just a little bit more, and helped individuals better appreciate the humanity that was represented there in the room, despite their political differences.

Quadrant Two: Discord—Survival of the Fittest!

Eventually, any collection of people who have been on their best behavior will begin to relax and "be themselves." At that point, behavior consistent with discord begins to appear. As we have seen in other examples, discord is not necessarily a negative quality. In fact, it is important to have some amount of it in order to know where the differences are and to get signs of what needs fixing. In the case example, some of the animosity between board members just bubbled to the surface, as one of the participants laid his emotions and anger on the table. He acknowledged some months later that he had felt comfortable doing it because he trusted that he would get the help he needed to frame his anger in a way that focused on the behavior rather than the individual, but it had the impact of breaking down the comfortable reserve and forcing participants to confront the raw emotion that was a constant accessory to their conflict. This was not an unfamiliar place, as we have already acknowledged, but it can still be a shock to experience the adversarialism in its full force.

This experience is a good example of the chaos that results from the parts each seeking their own separate states of equilibrium. It is a self-oriented place in which the parties are also self-protective. The main vulnerability that appears at this stage is the risk that is taken in attacking someone else. It is often blameful and tends to provoke defensive reactions in others. This can create a cycle of blame, in which one party credits another as the primary source of the problem. The more I am blamed, the more defensive I become, which makes me more blameful with others, and so the cycle continues. Perhaps most characteristic of this stage is the tendency for people to be preoccupied with advancing their own perspectives on the world. This can be a huge impediment to learning in an organization. For example, when a program turns up with a significant operating deficit, the initial reaction of key stakeholders is generally to make others wrong by naming their mismanagement or failure to provide the needed information, rather than just pitching in to figure out how to prevent the problem in the future. It is an important challenge for a leader in this situation to attempt to keep people from feeling or becoming blameful or defensive.

Typical of the often subtle dynamics of this stage is a story about a man who was frustrated by poor communications with his wife. The man had read somewhere that people become hard of hearing as they grow older, and he was convinced that he finally understood the source of their problems. But he decided to test his theory to be certain, and so he quietly entered the room behind his wife while she was reading. "Honey, can you hear me?" There was no response and so, moving closer, he tried again. "Honey, can you hear me?" Still nothing. Satisfied that his wife's poor hearing was the source of their problems, he decided to try one more time just to be sure, so he moved right up behind her and asked once again, "Honey, can you hear me?"

"For the third time, yes!" was her exasperated reply.

Often the discord in the second quadrant is the result of our own self-absorption. If we see conflict as a blameful situation that was created by others, then we see the solution lying in the hands of others as well. If we see the situation as a system created by our collective behavior and we prepare ourselves for the likelihood that each of us has some role in the process, then we begin to appreciate that conceiving a solution includes understanding our own contribution to the problem. Our conditioned reactions to stress promote that self-orientation and make it more difficult to open ourselves to the perspectives of others, even when we most need to be open. As Peck (1987) suggests, what is needed at this stage is to let go of our habitual viewpoint of how the world looks. The path to generative engagement lies only through that open, vulnerable, and self-reflective place.

Chapter 2, pages 19 and 20 includes another example of a group that was frozen for months in "Discord."

Quadrant Three: Introspection—Preparing to See the World Differently

A commitment to move past discord includes an obligation to engage in learning. So life in the third quadrant involves each of us understanding that, when I am involved in a conflict, there is relatively little I can do to influence others, but a whole lot that I can do to change myself. The path to generative working relationships in quadrant four often includes what threatens to be a painful, introspective journey through quadrant three. This process is introspective because it involves understanding the role that I am playing in our current dysfunction. It is potentially painful because it requires me to accept the possibility that I am engaging in behaviors that are contributing to the problem, at the very least by the way that my behavior is provoking you to act. The man's faulty test of his wife's hearing was a direct cause of her exasperation. This also means becoming vulnerable by opening up to critical feedback from others, which normally causes us to be defensive.

The school board in our example evolved naturally into introspection when we interrupted the blame cycle and asked the individuals to use inquiry skills to understand how each of their colleagues perceived the situation. This required us to identify the behaviors, and the subsequent thinking, that caused the perceived conflict. In this particular case, one board member perceived that another was deliberately interfering with his ability to advocate for the needs of his political constituency. Several others were greatly offended by the willingness of the first to make public what was seen as an interpersonal issue between two board members. An interesting conversation followed, which ultimately led to some concrete agreements about communication, and the most appropriate venue for surfacing and addressing conflicts.

See Chapter 7 for more information on how to apply the skills of inquiry in problem solving.

This third quadrant is the point at which learning is most likely to occur. It requires us to practice the qualities of openness that were described in Chapter 2, and it is vital to understand that it will *feel* like a very vulnerable process. We have been conditioned over a lifetime by our fight and flight responses to stress. Quadrant three represents a more enlightened and potentially powerful stage of our evolutionary response to conflict, because it does require our cognitive and rational brain functions to prevail over our emotional reactions. This is my opportunity to take in rational data that allows me to understand how my behavior and/or my assumptions interact with the behavior and assumptions of others to produce outcomes that impede the achievement of our shared vision.

I can illustrate this phenomenon with a personal example. I remember hearing once from an anonymous source that the true definition of a conservative is a father with teenage daughters, and that definition certainly applied to me when it came to my own children, despite any purported expertise I might have had in conflict resolution. I remember one particular conversation when I was carrying on relentlessly, as fathers are prone to do with their daughters. They listened patiently until I was finished, and then our oldest daughter asked me simply, "So, Dad, what are your interests?"

Her question brought me to an absolute halt, and may have helped me at that moment to transform my relationship with both of them. I realized that my true interests centered on their happiness and their safety, and I finally grasped the fact that I had long since passed the point at which I could or should control either of their lives. Both were legally adults by that point and both had already been living on their own, and yet I was clinging to an obsolete mental frame that cast me in the role of guardian and protector. By submitting my interests to their custody, I was transforming my relationship with each of them based on the kind of trust, respect, and understanding that everyone wanted. The experience was a little painful, because I needed to understand that my thinking was outdated and fear-based. I was also able to make a huge impact on the conflict we were experiencing simply by transforming the mindset that I brought to our relationships. The conflict simply went away.

Inevitably this process of reframing the mindset or assumptions that are contributing to the discord results in a new set of expectations for how people in the relationship should behave. This is the reason Tuckman (1965) calls this stage *norming* (p. 394), for it is necessary to reprogram the way individuals in the group interact in order to move to a high performing relationship. Peck (1987) calls it *emptiness* (pp. 209–225) because of the need for each individual to empty themselves of their assumptions and preconceived notions in order to form new mindsets as a community, rather than as individuals. The school board team eventually developed a set of operational agreements that helped their working relationships so much that a similar version was eventually adopted to govern interactions in the district as a whole. My own relationship with my daughters was transformed by a set of expectations that allowed me to give up any control I thought I had for a different kind of relationship. In the first example, everyone needed to agree to a new set of expectations. In the second, I was really the only one who needed to change. In doing so, my new way of seeing the world positively impacted the rest of the family and allowed all of us to interact in a more generative way.

See Chapter 6 for a discussion on the impact of assumptions on conflict and problem solving.

This is not to imply that discord is unhealthy. In Chapter 2, I used the example of the four cities working together to attempt to create a shared services agreement through their fire departments. Successful resolution required the group to understand and come to grips with their differences. Their inability to acknowledge and move past the differences had stymied their efforts to take any action at all. Ultimately they needed to organize their conversation in a way that allowed them to muck around enough in their problems for genuine learning to occur. Talking honestly about the "undiscussables" gave them the clarity they needed to learn and respond accordingly, including making it okay for some cities to drop out and for others to move on.

Quadrant Four: Generative Engagement—The Well-Aligned Team

Once the parties have allowed themselves to become open, vulnerable, and self-reflective enough to ensure that they are learning, and once their energy and attention have been focused on a shared vision, they tend to perform more effectively as a team. This is a state of being that permits collaboration and cocreation because participants are open to possibilities that will satisfy everyone's needs acceptably.

The school board team reached this stage of generative engagement by the end of the daylong retreat. They recognized that the future-oriented needs that they shared as a board were greater than the separate interests that each of them brought to the enterprise as discrete individuals. They used that alignment to generate a set of behavioral expectations that would allow them to function effectively as a team and to make plans that would advance their future work together. They were able to communicate appreciation of their respective points of view in a way that expressed understanding. This state of alignment is very similar to the condition achieved by the city council described in Chapter 1 that finally understood that they needed to pull themselves together in a way that would allow them to attract and ultimately hire a new city manager.

But generative engagement is a transitory state at best. The pull to stay closed and self-protective along with our fight and flight reactions tempt us to revert to compliance or discord at the first sign of conflict. It takes the mindful attention of every team member for the group to stay in this quadrant continuously. Adding new people, or simply a remark or event that triggers an emotional response as described in Chapter 2, can plunge them back into discord. Old habits that lead to discord run deep and are often difficult to extinguish. All too frequently groups that reach generative engagement with the support of an external facilitator or consultant will revert to discord when left to their own devices, unless there is a deliberate structure and plan to sustain the learning over time.

It becomes critical to create the day-to-day capacity in groups to organize meetings or daily interactions in a way that promotes alignment and, more important, that encourages a level of honesty and comfort needed to openly name and deal with the sources of discord that connect to interpersonal interactions as well as to the organizational mission. Similarly, those defenses that allow teams to perpetuate behaviors that block an open and honest flow of information must be detected and addressed.

Generative engagement capitalizes on the diverse perspectives and talents of a group that is committed to working together to find common ground and achieve shared goals. For example Fullan (2003) asserts the necessity for educators to work collaboratively together to ensure they are fulfilling the collective goal of "transforming the current school system so that large-scale, sustainable, continuous reform becomes built in" (p. 29). This can only happen when individuals have organized themselves to be able to maintain a laser-like focus on their collective vision. Collaborative organizational interactions require that all group members understand how their differing views of the world might be impacting each other's ability to work effectively together toward that greater good. At the heart of this reframing is a clear understanding that we live in a competitive culture in which our habits have been programmed toward adversarial behavior. It is easier for each of us to meet our own needs, let alone our collective ones, when there is no one actively opposing us. So we must mindfully attend to our own conduct as well as the conduct of others to ensure that it is consistent with our personal and collective visions of what we need to achieve and how we want to interact.

Summary

With our natural tendency to polarize competitively and adversarially when conflict is introduced, savvy leaders must be alert to opportunities to align the team by thoughtfully drawing the circle around all the stakeholders in the move to generative engagement. This is accomplished by understanding the stages of group development, and by taking the proactive steps necessary to keep all members open, vulnerable, and committed to maintaining a sense of community. These steps are described in detail in Part II of this book.

Before we move to an in-depth discussion of those aligning tools, it is important to understand the potentially negative side of the coherence principle. The same principles that enable us to create a consensus in an organization that allows us to collaboratively generate creative and powerful solutions to the thorniest problems also hold the capacity for implementing disastrous outcomes. An understanding and awareness of the perils of coherence can help ensure that we do not inadvertently implement decisions that will undermine or sabotage an organization's vision and reason for being. This is the focus of Chapter 4.

CHAPTER FOUR

The Perils of Coherence

Bad Agreements, False Coherence, and Groupthink

As we explored in Chapter 3, there are important qualities that are generally present in highly effective groups, and a variety of conditions can disrupt those dynamics. Whether it is the departure or arrival of a key individual, interpersonal animosities, changing political, economic, or market conditions, or labor unrest, almost anything can send the organization back into discord, and so adaptability is the key to survival. Popular organizational authors like Peters (1987), Land and Jarman (1992), and Stacey (1992) are increasingly championing the notion that the teams and organizations most able to flourish in these tumultuous and unpredictable times are the ones most able to thrive on conflict, chaos, and uncertainty, while maintaining their organizational focus. An ability to effectively bring teams to agreement in times of significant conflict has some real advantages for leaders in this complex world.

But there is a dark side to our natural tendencies to align ourselves, and effective leaders wishing to exploit the benefits of coherence must also be mindfully aware of the dangers. This chapter will consider some of those pitfalls, which will in turn provide important background and context to the tools that will follow in Part II of this book.

A NATURAL RESISTANCE TO CHANGE

I worked with an organization many years ago that had developed some interpersonal dynamics that I have seen repeated many times since. A respected but highly autocratic school superintendent had retired. He was celebrated as a "charismatic hero," and decisions throughout the district under his leadership tended to be top-down and highly centralized. As often happens in a transition like this one, the school board asked for input from the rest of the organization on what qualities they should consider in a successor. Consequently they recruited and eventually hired a superintendent with a collaborative approach who would encourage much more active involvement in decision making from participants throughout the district.

The new leader was warmly welcomed to the fold, and his tenure promised to be a happy and amicable one. A colleague and I came in to build capacity for collaborative problem solving, and we expected to see the tools and attitudes flourish. But a funny thing happened on the road to collaboration. All the decision making that the superintendent was trying to share, and that managers had clamored for, was being delegated upward again, right back to the CEO. A closer look revealed some of the reasons. No one was used to going out on a limb. The culture was very risk averse, because the former boss had discouraged initiative for so many years that few were willing to chance being wrong, and there was comfort in the paternalism they had resented for the preceding years.

It is not so unusual for individuals to ultimately resist the very thing that had been most desired. Lord Byron's poem "The Prisoner of Chillon" details the long and unjust captivity of the title character. Even with an unfair and capricious imprisonment, the inmate becomes comfortable enough with so many years in the harsh but familiar surroundings that "even I regain'd my freedom with a sigh" (Byron, 1904, p. 340). As attractive as the desired state had once seemed, what is customary and familiar is also appealing.

Similarly, our superintendent discovered with some consternation that the ingrained habits of autocracy had their own appeal for the subordinates. At a deep level, there was a certain comfort with the way things were, and a deep resistance to the kind of change and risk that collaboration really required. There was something to grumble about, and no one needed to take responsibility for anything. Coherence had been created at that deeper level around the status quo, and the new superintendent needed to initiate a profound realignment around the kinds of values, qualities, and attitudes that would be needed to achieve the workplace relationships he had been hired to promote.

WHEN ALIGNMENT LEADS TO GRIEF

The pattern that this district was experiencing occurs often when an organization encounters change and fails to bring about the kind of cultural modifications that will enable it to realign. Alignment in the form of compliance is often created through the use of power and intimidation, and the habits that go with it can be difficult to break. This is the reason that many groups or families are codependent to self-destructive or abusive behavior. We are so sensitive to collective opinion that we will go to great lengths to ignore the discord and to realign ourselves in a way that tolerates the negative behavior in order to preserve a semblance of alignment to each other and to the outside world.

How Codependence Leads to Compliance

People fear discord, and so the undiscussables take the form of the "elephant in the parlor," which is tacitly accepted, rather than confronting and changing the behavior. Sometimes this occurs when the members of an organization rewire themselves to function effectively in lieu of a key leader. One public sector organization considered their boss to be so vindictive and unstable that they created alternative decision making mechanisms to get most issues resolved without ever bringing her into the loop. The organization functioned well enough on a day-to-day basis, but had problems responding to the strategic challenges that required visionary leadership from the chief executive.

This is an organization that had aligned itself into a culture of compliance through codependence. Fearful of the chaos, conflict, or retribution that might come from openly and honestly addressing the negative behavior that was plaguing them, the members of the organization settled into a closed, self-protective existence, rather than risking the kind of discussion that might improve everyone's lives and enhance the effectiveness of the organization. This kind of negative alignment is often in place in departments, in schools, or in broader organizations. Until someone has the courage and the skill to name and address the problem, it is destined to continue indefinitely. This is an example of an *organizational defensive routine* as described in Chapter 2.

Alignment is not a virtue if it goes against the core values of group members. History is filled with examples in which a group creates an alignment that permits or condones behavior that runs contrary to basic human values. This might apply to apartheid, U.S. race relations, Watergate, ethnic cleansing policies in the former Yugoslav republics, the atrocities that took place in Nazi Germany, or a mentality that condones "creative" accounting in corporate business practices. Each of these examples represents a situation in which ordinary people appeared to accept negative behavior either out of agreement, fear, or ignorance.

This produces compliance, which is the self-protective but community oriented quadrant that is reflected in Figure 3.4. This alignment represents false coherence, because it reflects what people are willing to tolerate from a "don't rock the boat" perspective rather than revealing what they truly want. For example, I reflect painfully to this day on my own involvement as a boy in a prank or two that I knew could be hurtful to someone else, and yet tolerated out of my own childish weakness. Unfortunately, grief can flow in the world, including the workplace, from compliant acceptance of conditions and behavior that violates our true vision of how the world should look. Understanding how to reach good agreements in groups must necessarily include knowing how to avoid bad ones.

It's What's Inside That Counts

Figure 3.4 suggests that a group that achieves a community orientation is not necessarily an effectively functioning team. Many long-standing teams, like the ones described in this chapter, are characterized by a compliance orientation on the part of participants, who may be community oriented on the outside, but who internally approach life and their organizations from a place of fear.

Table 4.1 compares the internal qualities that are in place for groups in compliance and those in generative engagement. Like the portion of an iceberg that lies below the surface of the water, these internal qualities are less easily visible to outsiders who glimpse the organization from a distance. But a closer analysis will reveal the

Table 4.1   Internal Attitudes and Behaviors in a Community Orientation

Generative Engagement	Compliance
Individualistic and flexible	Prescribed behavior
Contributions tend to look different	Contributions tend to look the same
Mindfulness	Habit based
Long-range strategic vision	Short-term, tactical vision
Self-monitoring accountability for behavior based on the shared vision	Codependent toleration of off-vision behavior. Accountability to outside hierarchy
Thriving on chaos and discord	Fear of chaos and discord

kinds of behaviors that either promote or impede effective team performance. A group that exhibits the qualities of compliance may be aligned in the sense that all the members of the team behave in a way that allows them to continue in that mode. Unfortunately, that alignment may actually be incoherent because those behaviors tend to be closed, defensive, and self-protective, rather than well aligned to deliver the organization's vision.

When Fear Aligns the Department: A Case Study

The predicament of one city's human resources (HR) department illustrates this situation. This group, like the rest of the city, was being prodded by the city manager to function collaboratively and to deliver a very high level of customer service. But there were numerous complaints from the department's "customers," in this case the other departments in the city, that their HR needs were not being well met. Specifically, recruitment and advertising for positions was too slow, paperwork was taking too long, training services were unresponsive to department needs, and there was a general resentment that the department was just too mired in bureaucracy and department members were generally too slow in responding to requests and getting the work done.

A closer look at the individual behaviors and attitudes revealed a department with internal qualities that mirror the ones listed in the right-hand column of Table 4.1. Interviews with individual members of the department were characterized by numerous perceptions of fear. People were fearful that their jobs were in jeopardy if they could not successfully address problems they saw all around them.

They were also afraid to go too far out on a limb, believing that those before them had been fired for being wrong and that it was too easy to make mistakes trying to meet the needs of their assertive and particular customers. The group's focus seemed to be on survival, and many long-time members of the department had survived quite a while doing business the same way, delegating difficult decisions upward, and waiting to be told which of the many hot issues on their plates needed the most attention.

Managers in the HR department, and in other departments, became increasingly annoyed with the behavior, so they responded with more directive behavior, which reinforced the system that was the most frustrating. Everyone's behavior was in alignment, but almost everyone was upset with the status quo. People blamed each other for the situation, and few seemed able to take responsibility for the broader vision, and for making things work more effectively. Although changes in management produced significant differences in management style, those differences seemed to cause little variation in the output of the department or in the perception of the other departments who were its customers. The unit only seemed to respond to mandates from the city or department hierarchies.

The internal behavior of individual members of the department determined the nature of the alignment that occurred. Behavior was self-protective and habitual, and there seemed to be little cultural encouragement of the kind of proactive problem solving and risk-taking that comes with generative engagement.

THE DANGERS OF GROUPTHINK

The mindful effort of members of a group to align their thinking in ways that allow them to find common ground and resolve problems effectively is not without risk. If the members of a group are too eager in their desire to find consensus, they are in danger of becoming victims of *groupthink*, which has been defined as:

A mode of thinking that people engage in when they are deeply involved in a cohesive in-group, when the members' strivings for unanimity override their motivation to realistically appraise alternative courses of action . . . Groupthink refers to a deterioration of mental efficiency, reality testing, and moral judgment that results from in-group pressures. (Janis, 1983, p. 9)

Our efforts to produce agreement in groups can lead to disaster if we are uninformed about the dangers and causes of groupthink. Irving Janis (1983) formulated the concept in his analysis of a variety of historically important domestic and foreign policy fiascoes as well as successes, and he made a case for how the learning can be translated to decision making in organizations. Janis categorized the symptoms of groupthink into three different types (as identified in Table 4.2), and those qualities convey the sense of a coherence among participants that may actually undermine the true interests of the organization.

When these symptoms are scrutinized more closely, we recognize that attitudes and skills that help to create true coherence will also serve to safeguard against groupthink. Figure 3.4 emphasized the importance of maintaining attitudes of *openness* and *vulnerability*, versus the closed and self-protective approaches of *compliance* and *discord*. A focus on learning will at least help to safeguard against implementing decisions based on faulty perceptions or ill-conceived assumptions. Recognizing that any decision has the potential to be a product of groupthink and thoughtfully honoring dissent related to the rightness of the cause or course of action can help to ensure that an effort to align a group does not become a mindless march toward failure. Though it happens everywhere in organizations, we see the groupthink phenomenon surprisingly often in labor relations. For example, several years ago a businessman told me the story of an

Table 4.2   Symptoms of Groupthink According to Janis

Type I: Overestimation of the group:
1. Illusion of invulnerability
2. Unquestioned belief in inherent morality

Type II: Closed-mindedness:
3. Rationalization to discount warnings or other disconfirming information
4. Stereotyped views of "enemies" or rivals

Type III: Pressures toward uniformity
5. Self-censorship of opinions deviating from the norm
6. Shared illusion of unanimity, including the false assumption that silence means consent
7. Direct pressure on dissenters
8. Self-appointed mind guards who protect the group from disconfirming evidence related to the effectiveness of their decisions

SOURCE: Janis (1983, pp. 174–175).

unprofitable regional newspaper that was up for sale, and a potential buyer approached the union to negotiate productivity improvements. While the paper had already purchased the technology needed to fully computerize the layout processes, none was in service because of the concern of the union that such innovations inevitably lead to a loss of jobs. The new buyer asked the union leadership to reconsider, and after conferring internally and convinced of the correctness of its approach, the union reasserted its opposition to negotiating any changes that would lead to a loss of jobs. The potential buyer thanked the union for its honesty, and declined to purchase the paper. The owner, who had no other prospective buyers, filed for bankruptcy and closed the paper. Instead of losing some jobs, all of them were lost. This closed-minded and overconfident estimate of the situation happens often on both sides of the bargaining table. It is not unusual for leaders to head dauntlessly into strike situations, sometimes overconfident about their ability to prevail, and neglecting to scrutinize their own role in creating the conditions that are leading to the strike.

THE MINDFUL PREVENTION OF BAD AGREEMENTS

By now we are realizing how easy it is to substitute an artificial alignment for authentic coherence based on thoughtful commitment to the vision and values of the organization and its members. There is a real danger that coherence will be wrongly or mistakenly claimed when, in fact, there is none. Anyone who aspires to lead groups to agreements should be mindful how difficult the gauntlet can be that separates a group from a good agreement, and should be aware of how to avoid the pitfalls. Table 4.3 lists four likely causes that can create an unproductive or destructive version of alignment.

RUSH TO JUDGMENT

Sometimes a rush to judgment in our haste to achieve coherence causes us to take shortcuts that lead us to very bad agreements. NASA's eagerness to launch the ill-fated space shuttle *Challenger* in January of 1986 was due in large measure to a desire to silence the critics who were embarrassing them about repeated delays on the

Table 4.3   Causes of False Coherence

Causes of False Coherence
1. Rush to judgment
2. Fear of looking bad or thinking differently, or an inability to challenge conventional thinking
3. Unclear goals or vision
4. Inertia or inaction

high profile mission. NASA's hurry is suggested by the response of the manager of the solid rocket booster program when he heard the engineers of Morton Thiokol, the manufacturer of the booster, recommending a launch delay due to the low temperatures anticipated for launch day. "My God, Morton Thiokol! When do you want me to launch—next April?" (Hauptman & Iwaki, 1990, p. 12)

A city council member also shared a story with me of how his council paid a high monetary price for rushing to judgment. The city was rebuilding a park, and the idea of adding a parking lot to the project seemed to make good sense at the time, because it was expected to attract users from other parts of the city. The council jumped on the idea, and a portion of the park was quickly torn out to make way for parking. By the time the neighbors understood what was happening to this segment of the park, the paving had already started. There was uproar over the issue, and eventually the council ended up reversing itself, tearing out the changes that had been made, and restoring the park. The cost of installing and then removing the parking lot came to nearly half a million dollars. In its haste to implement what had seemed like a good idea, the council overlooked the potential reaction of the community, which obviously mattered a great deal to them based on their ultimate reversal. Slowing decision making enough to ensure that all the critical perspectives and information are available to the deciders can tremendously improve the staying power of a decision over time.

FEAR OF THINKING DIFFERENTLY

The members of a group or organization frequently remain closed and self-protective because of the perception that open behavior and

Figure 4.1   Asch's Experiment

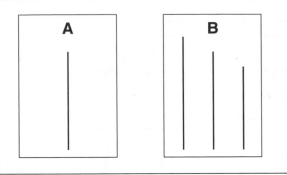

risk taking will be punished rather than encouraged. Group members' fears can vary from concern about looking bad, to apprehensions about authority, or an unwillingness to be different.

Solomon Asch demonstrated this phenomenon in a famous experiment in which subjects were shown two cards represented in Figure 4.1 and asked to identify which line in B is the same length as the line in A. In each group tested there was only one true subject. The others were assistants to the experimenter who were told how to answer. The subject was always asked to respond last.

When the confederates in the experiment gave the same wrong answer, 74% of the subjects were induced to give at least one wrong answer to go along with the group. The average subject conformed to the group response on 32% of the trials. No one made errors when they were tested alone without the influence of the confederates. Clearly there is an incredibly strong urge to conform, even when our perceptions indicate that our conforming response is an incorrect one (Dobson, Hardy, Heyes, A. Humphreys, & P. Humphreys,1981).

The impact of Asch's studies on leaders striving to build consensus is huge. There is an aspect of human nature inclined to conform to a group, even when we feel everyone else in the group is wrong. In order to combat this, a group aspiring to create positive coherence needs to cultivate an expectation that it values dissent; moreover, it needs to foster behaviors that make that value operational. That means encouraging group members to take enough time to disagree when they feel things are headed in the wrong direction, and to expect that dissent to trigger a healthy, thoughtful dialogue without fear of intimidation or reprisal.

How Groups Become Autocratic

This becomes particularly critical, and difficult, when the group is subject to autocratic behavior that is actively creating this pressure to conform. It is also my experience that autocratic pressure to behave in a certain way comes as often from the collective staff as it does from a given leader. There can be a great deal of pressure on new staff members to conform to the general expectations of the group, which tends to stifle the energy and innovation that is so badly needed.

As I was conducting individual assessment interviews with staff members of one elementary school, I learned of a pervasive perception on the part of new faculty members as well as some veteran observers that new staff were often "taken under the wing" of more experienced teachers and taught the ways of the school. The indoctrination included specific instructions on what kinds of teaching approaches were acceptable, how to behave toward staff, parents, and administration, and other guidelines for acceptable collegial behavior. While this mentoring would normally be considered to be a very useful orientation to the culture of the school and a helpful way to ensure that new staff members felt included, it was perceived to have the unfortunate effect and intent in this situation of suppressing the creativity and energy that new people can bring to a team. Some cynics felt that the expressed intent was to ensure that the new staff members did not engage in high-energy activities that would somehow make other staff members look bad if they did not behave the same way. The result, if true, would be to stifle creativity and innovation.

This pattern is repeated often in schools and other organizations. Teams need to develop expectations that the culture is open to negotiation at all times if anyone has an idea for improving "the way we do things around here." This means developing a healthy dialogue about what works and what does not, and ways of learning and improving how staff go about the business of the organization. It means living comfortably in the third quadrant of "reframing" in Figure 3.4, and seeking out dissent if it is not forthcoming. Organizations must actively search for disconfirming evidence that suggests better ways of operating, rather than waiting for a courageous soul to risk rocking the boat that is not used to being disturbed.

Knowing When Not to Move On

It also means that leaders must go back to instability if they sense that the agreement that is being cultivated is inauthentic. A manager in a city told a story about a time when he was facilitating a meeting of city staff and massage therapists on changes to the massage ordinance. On one issue everyone was in agreement except one therapist, who said he would go along with the group. But the facilitator sensed that the hesitant therapist was really upset about the decision. Even though there seemed to be consensus, the facilitator wondered whether to proceed or spend more time exploring and reconciling his additional concerns. Should he spend some more time making sure that "Jerry" felt heard, or should he leave well enough alone by pushing on to the next issue?

However tempting it is to take an agreement and run when you have it in hand, it may prove to be more work in the long run if it is a false alignment. The manager decided to check back with Jerry to make sure that he could at least live with the agreement, or to determine what it would take to improve the agreement to make it acceptable for "Jerry." Despite the fear of prolonging what otherwise seems like a legitimate outcome, it is important to find some mechanism for tapping into the wisdom of the "Jerrys" in our midst. If for some reason it can't be done openly in the group, then a break could be requested and Jerry could be asked privately about his lingering concerns. When it comes to encouraging dissent, the only fear that can really be tolerated is a fear of complacency, and of not taking every possible opportunity to learn and improve any given decision.

UNCLEAR GOALS OR VISION

One of the greatest sources of misalignment in a group comes from the group allowing itself to press forward on an agreement when it has been focusing on the wrong goals. The *Challenger* tragedy resulted, in part, from the erroneous preoccupation by the NASA team with public relations concerns (as it turns out) at the cost of their interests in safety. Had safety been the highest priority focus, it is unlikely that a decision would have been made to proceed at those cold temperatures, despite the warnings of experts on their own team about the dangers of launching. Tragically, the same dynamics have been determined to be the cause of the disaster leading to the loss of the *Columbia* shuttle 17 years later. The report of the Columbia Accident Investigation Board (2003) finds that:

> NASA's safety culture has become reactive, complacent, and dominated by unjustified optimism. Over time, slowly and unintentionally, independent checks and balances intended to increase safety have been eroded in favor of detailed processes that produce massive amounts of data and unwarranted consensus, but little effective communication. Organizations that successfully deal with high-risk technologies create and sustain a disciplined safety system capable of identifying, analyzing, and controlling hazards throughout a technology's life cycle (p. 180).

What this classic example of negative coherence teaches us is how critical it is to understand our core interests, and to be sure that the decisions that we make are clearly focused on helping us to fulfill those basic priorities.

In Chapter 3, I mentioned a colleague who, as a city manager, constantly strives to help his council reach consensus solutions. He shared a wonderful example with me of how this philosophy allowed his council to avoid a decision that promised to be a bad one. One council member wanted to name a walking trail after a former mayor and local educator who had given a great deal of service to the community. The council member had two others who would support the idea and wanted to move the issue quickly to a decision.

The problem was that the other two council members felt that another former councilman had been far more instrumental in creating the shoreline. A vote at that point would have not only put them in the very uncomfortable position of voting against the proposal but also given a very negative spin to an event that was intended to be a tribute. They were very glad to honor the former teacher and mayor, but didn't feel that the walking trail had much to do with the work in the community for which he was

See Chapter 7 for more on how to keep a focus on the vision in problem solving and decision making.

most remembered. In the end, after a thorough analysis of the interests, they voted 5 to 0 to name a street in his honor that passed in front of the school in which he had worked for more than 30 years. They were able to develop a solution that was not only more appropriate as a tribute to their former colleague, but that also avoided an outcome with negative votes that would have significantly tarnished the honor.

I told the story in Chapter 3 of my own journey of discovery as a parent of two daughters making their way to adulthood. When my actions were focused on maintaining control of their behavior, we were all frequently "off vision" and my own behavior even undermined many of the elements of that vision that I really held most dear. When I returned to the vision, and the core interests around which it was constructed, I realized that the only way to ensure a loving, trusting, and respectful relationship—as well as their safety, happiness, and self-sufficiency—was to turn over "control" of their lives to them. As discussed in Chapter 3, I really wasn't giving up a thing; by then they were both legally adults and I probably had not had "control" for years.

INERTIA OR INACTION

Perhaps the most subtle and dangerous source of negative alignment in groups is the one that is brought about by inertia or inaction. A willingness to search relentlessly for solutions is a critical component to working through an impasse, and if that dogged determination to find the solution is lacking in a group, then the entire group just languishes in the status quo, however miserable and unacceptable that condition may feel. This recalls "The Prisoner of Chillon," whose liberation from a harsh imprisonment was described at the beginning of this chapter. However intolerable the circumstances may seem, there can be comfort in its familiarity that somehow discourages proactively addressing the situation in order to make things better. I recall a lengthy conversation with the members of a department who were extremely unhappy with the behavior of the department head. When pressed whether they had used any of a number of avenues that were available to them to call attention to the situation, they replied with a chorus of reasons why they had not:

"It wouldn't make any difference anyway."

"Our boss is so clueless that we're better off this way."

"We don't really want any changes because we work fine together the way things are, without any help from our boss."

"Why go to all that trouble to try to fix someone who will
retire anyway in a couple of years."

This was not a powerless collection of people who were inca-
pable of addressing a thorny problem like this one. Some were
skilled communicators and problem solvers caught in a group mindset that it is better to suffer the status quo than to risk the chaos that
results from raising and addressing "undiscussable" problems. In
fact, not long after this discussion, some of the staff members did
take advantage of an opportunity to open the conversation, and so the
wheels were set in motion to resolve the situation.

Similarly, a group at an impasse is often waiting for someone to
identify and resolve the deadlock, and that wait can sometimes last
a long time. Often a mediator to a labor or workplace dispute plays
little more than a catalyst's role to force the participants to walk
through the problem solving process that is introduced in the
chapters that follow. Nothing changes other than the introduction of
a change agent who forces the individuals who have already been
parties to the dispute to start generating solutions to address the
identified needs. I have also observed numerous situations in
which that mediating role is played by
an internal facilitator, like the boss or
another member of the team. Invariably
the breakthrough ideas come from the
participants themselves; in fact, I can
remember few, if any, instances in

*For more information on
dealing with impasse, see
Chapter 9.*

which a group of individuals, who were all persistently committed to
finding a solution, had adequate knowledge of effective group process
strategies, and were in the room to support consensus, were unsuccessful. All that is required is energy for the task, a willingness by
participants to get their hands dirty working hard to find an acceptable solution, and an understanding of how to apply some basic tools
for creating coherence.

SUMMARY

Understanding how to respond effectively and proactively to change
means understanding the benefits of discord in a relationship, as well
as the dangers that come with members of a group aligning to create

a bad solution or situation. While a modern organizational leader must become comfortable with the landscape of conflict in order to induce the organization to self-organize to achieve some degree of order, there must also be an understanding of the signs that can lead to a bad agreement.

Any accord should be purposeful, thoughtfully crafted, free of fear and intimidation, and focused on the core needs of stakeholders. Leaders can foster the courage and the critical thinking that is needed to ensure that people are able to challenge one another to move authentically in the right direction, based on a genuine understanding of their morality, values, and interests. The very same skills can be applied when a false coherence is detected, to move the group to a place of alignment that is truly consistent with those core values. Part II of this book begins with Chapter 5 and a description of the fundamental elements for creating positive coherence.

PART II

Tools and Strategies for Leading Through Collaboration

Part I of this book discussed the habits and attitudes that are necessary for an aspiring leader to take responsibility for guiding an organization through a collaborative process of ongoing improvement. Part II represents the how-to manual of tools and strategies that make it possible for leaders to create shared meaning in their teams as they utilize the principles of coherence to produce excellent and enduring agreements. These tools offer an approach to creating and problem solving that is based on members of the team taking responsibility for engaging in a joint search for solutions that strives to address everyone's needs effectively.

There are certain stages that define that search for clear, compliance-prone, and mutually acceptable results to problems and to conflict. These stages are summarized in Chapter 5, and each is the subject of a subsequent chapter in which the skills are detailed. While there is no recipe for exactly how to move a group to collaborative agreements, these stages offer a progression to move logically and methodically from the identification of a situation through to the resolution and development of commitments. More important, a process that reflects the thinking and commands the ownership of the diverse stakeholders is much more likely to produce results that will be implemented.

CHAPTER FIVE

The Fundamental Elements for Creating Coherence

THE FACILITATIVE LEADER

The four fundamental elements for creating coherence that are the focus of this part of the book have been inspired by some long traditions that run through the literature of organizational peace-making. The pioneering work of Mary Parker Follett, who articulated the concepts of *revaluation* and *integration* in the 1920s, lies somewhere at the root of it all. She pointed out that a natural process of "revaluing our desires" in the context of conflict allows interests to fit together so that everyone's core needs are adequately addressed (Follett, 1940, pp. 30–50). Follett's approach to conflict has become something of a worldwide standard thanks to the popular book *Getting to Yes* (Fisher & Ury, 1981) that followed over a half century later.

These four fundamentals (which are listed below in Table 5.1) should be familiar elements of the coherence principle I have described in Part I. Each reflects a holistic attitude that allows a leader to serve as a process steward whose primary purpose is to support the work of a group in such a way that its members achieve a synergy that enables them to get the work done well, and to ensure that everyone's interests are effectively served. Acquired en masse with the appropriate tools, they offer some powerful skills for producing agreements in groups of all kinds.

Table 5.1   The Four Fundamentals

1. Aligning the Team

2. Focusing on the Vision

3. Searching for Solutions

4. Reaching Agreements

ALIGNING THE TEAM

Most great teachers work diligently to create a classroom environment that is attractive to students, that stimulates thinking and learning in a variety of ways, and that encourages students to interact effectively with each other and the teacher. This thorough preparation also includes identifying and transmitting the rules and conditions that will govern mutually supportive learning and getting clarity on the learning tasks and how they will be achieved. The time and attention that is lavished on creating an effective learning environment is vital. Few good teachers would overlook the exhaustive groundwork that is needed to ensure a quality learning experience, because a poorly prepared classroom is an invitation to educational mayhem.

But take a staff full of such enlightened educators and throw them together in a meeting, and it is not unusual to encounter interactions that are remarkably unhelpful to the mutual learning of the adults in the organization. Often little thought is given to where folks will sit, who does what, how topics or issues are organized and addressed, and what strategies are used to address them. An effective meeting, like an excellent lesson, requires the same thoughtful attention to detail, well before the members of the team get together to begin their work.

This preparatory process requires attention to the conditions in which problems are addressed. Leaders must ensure that participants are focused on common goals, have clear expectations, and that everyone is pitching in for the good of the whole and hanging together when things get tough. Assumptions are explicitly checked, so that everyone who interacts in that setting understands what is expected and how they should be behaving.

There is a procedural piece of this in problem solving that involves clarifying the task and keeping participants open so that there is enough alignment to ensure that participants are attacking the same problems and not each other. I have discovered over the years that groups predisposed to working inclusively with one another really begin to flourish when they are introduced to these tools and concepts.

On the other hand, once a space is created for a team, its members must remain vigilant to the likelihood that a variety of factors can contribute to deterioration over time. I have worked for a number of years with labor-management teams that endeavor to collaboratively manage the relationship and address key issues in the department or organization. The most successful teams regularly schedule "tune-ups," either as a preventative measure or to address the discord that inevitably seems to creep back into the relationship.

FOCUSING ON THE VISION

As we explored in Part I, it is normal behavior in a conflict to first decide how to address an issue that involves others, and then to devote a lot of effort trying to figure out how to get "the other guy" to go along. The process of creating coherence requires an inquiry approach to problem solving, which means that problem solvers must put questions ahead of answers. The core values of the stakeholders need to be clarified and understood in advance of the search for solutions so that the group's collective energy can be devoted to finding a resolution that satisfies those requirements. This necessarily involves separating the interests from the positions so the focus is on core needs rather than preconceived outcomes.

I do use interests, values, and vision somewhat interchangeably. A powerful vision will provide a beacon to a group in the form of collective and separate interests that are driving the members of the organization to work together toward a common goal. Awareness of those "reasons for being" will ensure that decisions made and actions taken are on target. This also necessarily involves checking regularly to ensure that the stated vision is valid and relevant to changing needs and conditions.

Sometimes groups just lose sight of the big picture by overlooking what is most important to them. I worked periodically with a small elementary school program that comprises dedicated teachers and highly supportive parents. Our first intervention with this community involved creating a space for staff to address some competitive and adversarial behaviors that had crept into their collegial relationships.

Even parents had encouraged the staff to get together, because of a realization that the negativity was affecting the quality of instruction to students. Staff members were quickly able to affirm a collective vision of an outstanding program delivered by a high-trust team that communicated together respectfully, in a way that nurtured trustfulness and respect over time.

After this brief intervention, the teachers were again performing as a cohesive team. However, a couple of years later some of the same competitive dynamics began to surface between staff members and parents. Each was questioning the other's motives and acting in a way that eroded the trust and raised doubt about commitment to the program. A series of disrespectful comments, letters, and third party conversations underscored the hostility and doubt that had surfaced, and that friction was jeopardizing the entire program. Once again leaders of both groups agreed to sit down together to address the conflict and validate the core vision that had attracted parents and staff to the program in the first place. They soon remembered that they had common goals for the program and their relationships, and they were able to reaffirm their willingness to behave in a way that would stay focused on the commitment to the collective vision.

This is not to say that the focus is always on common interests. Rigorous advocacy for a group's uniquely separate needs is vital to producing an acceptable solution. More important, an individual becomes a more powerful problem solver and negotiator by learning to understand and address the needs of others, even traditional adversaries. An ability to understand what is important to every significant stakeholder, and to figure out viable solutions that address those needs is a skill that is vital to modern organizational life. A member of an organization who learns to do it well becomes a most powerful problem solver.

SEARCHING FOR SOLUTIONS

When there is an ability to know and understand what really motivates key stakeholders, the search for a resolution can become a joint search for approaches that will effectively meet all the identified needs. The most critical attitude involved in that search is a commitment to learning, which is essentially willingness to end the search with an entirely different perspective than when it began.

For example, the union and management leaders in a school district were able to avert grievances and legal action in a situation in which the state had disallowed credits that had been granted by the district over many years for salary schedule placement. The leaders worked together with local universities to create an on-site master's degree program to make it possible for teachers whose salaries would be adversely impacted to make up the credits and earn advanced degrees in the process. This solution was only possible because the leaders of both groups were well aligned in their interests and their desired approach to the problem. This alignment allowed the leaders of both groups to remain undistracted by their constituents' anger. Instead they came together to find a solution that would address everyone's needs, including those of the state.

This search for solutions requires the same mindset of openness discussed in Chapter 3. The union leadership in the school district described above could have sat back pointing fingers of blame and bashing the district leadership on whose watch the mistake had compounded. Instead everyone realized that the problem created a great opportunity, and so the internal academy was created. Relentlessly following the learning led to an open search for new approaches that significantly improved the professional development opportunities in the district.

REACHING AGREEMENTS

People will often complain, "I'm really not a process person. I just like to get things done." In fact, the very reason to use these process tools is to ensure that things do get done, and that they have a chance to get done well and with everyone's buy-in. While collaborative approaches fulfill an important community-building function in public organizations, that benefit is a bonus. The reason they should be used in the first place is because of the potential they offer to deliver better results to the "customers," and that means efficiently reaching great agreements.

The move to closure must include consideration of what should happen to bring a group to completion once a promising list of possibilities has been identified. The work of the facilitative leader is never really done. Not only does she create a space in which alignment is possible, she ensures that the vision is clearly defined, and that there is a thoughtful search for solutions that culminates with an acceptable and viable outcome. Like the relationship itself, that outcome must be monitored well into the future to ensure that it is implemented as intended.

The notion of learning also goes far beyond the search for solutions. Ample opportunity for reflection and improvement is critical to ensure that an organization and its activities remain vital. I hear an adage repeated anywhere I go to work with public employees, "We have to redesign our plane at the same time that we're flying it." There is so little time allocated to research and development in the public sector, that organizational learners must develop habits that enable them to continually monitor and improve their efforts toward change.

The staff in one elementary school understood this need so powerfully that they committed to a guiding norm that would ensure that they will hold one another accountable to continually engage in conversations focused on reflection and learning. For them, this meant building action-learning opportunities into every meeting, as well as the implementation plans for every new program. This emphasis on reflection also has a very pragmatic side. It is much easier for me to say "yes" to the resolution of a dispute if I can be certain that there will be a meaningful opportunity to evaluate the solution over time and to improve it if it doesn't adequately address my needs.

A PROCESS FOR PROBLEM SOLVING AND NEGOTIATIONS

The four fundamentals described above will serve the humanistic leader well in any circumstance. But they also have many practical applications, and the next four chapters will detail those tools and attitudes that make these components effective and useful. Figure 5.1 offers a framework for problem solving with these attitudes and skills.

Open Things Up Before Closing Them Down

There has been much discussion here about the value of openness, and that value certainly applies to the process of problem solving. The primary focus is taking steps to ensure that problem solvers do not get locked into a favorite, familiar, or habit-based way

Figure 5.1   A Framework for Creating Coherence in Problem Solving

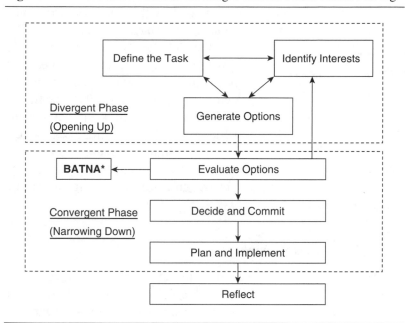

NOTE: *BATNA = Best Alternative To a Negotiated Agreement

of approaching a problem. This necessarily involves organizing the approach to ensure that the process is divergent (opening up) before it converges (narrows down) to a solution. Figure 5.1 illustrates how those phases fit into a problem solving framework. Each of the components of Figure 5.1 fits into one of the fundamental elements described above, and in the following chapters.

BATNA (Best Alternative to a Negotiated Agreement)

The framework separates the processes of creating and evaluating. The divergent phase provides an opportunity to create a problem solving relationship and tell the story in a way that clarifies the task, understands the underlying motivations that distinguish each of the stakeholders, and creates options that are uniquely designed to address the identified needs. The convergent phase allows an opportunity for the problem solvers to narrow the range of possibilities in the context of the interests, and to fashion a solution together that has great promise of being agreeable, successful, and capable of implementation. In the convergent phase, the framework will be compared not only against the identified interests, but also to what Fisher and Ury (1981) call the *BATNA* (Best Alternative To a Negotiated Agreement), which each of the parties will choose on their own if there is no agreement (p. 104). The framework is designed to keep participants working together off a single page, rather than competing with each other by designing separate approaches. The leader is the steward of this process, guiding participants through the divergent and convergent phases in a way that brings them to a successful agreement.

> *BATNA is further described in the example below and in Chapter 9.*

A High-Stakes Example

These concepts are detailed in the chapters that follow, but an example will help to describe how the framework typically operates. Our own family found ourselves plunged into conflict many years ago when the older of our two daughters, who was then 14, was a freshman in high school. One day she announced that "David," a 17-year-old student, asked her out to the movies. We should have anticipated this situation but we did not think she had shown much interest in romance up to that point, and, as a typical father, I certainly had no intention of encouraging it. Our reaction as parents was also somewhat predictable—we were fearful, emphatic, and positional in our opposition.

The emotional scene that followed may also have been predictable, and it was enough to convince my wife and me that we had entered a new era in our lives as parents, and that if we did not embrace this conflict we were looking at a rocky road ahead. As we contemplated the future, we realized that our failure to address this issue would lead to the situation repeating itself continually into the future, or worse yet, we glimpsed a future in which we were alienated from our daughter—a very unacceptable prospect. This was ample motivation to engage in a discussion, so we sat down with both our daughters and we started to problem solve. The divergent phase of the journey had already started for me, as I realized that life—as I knew it with my daughters—was shifting and that I needed to reframe how, as a father, I interacted with our changing brood.

Table 5.2   Approach to Dating Interests

Daughters	Parents
A. Have fun →	← A. Safety
B. Respect →	B. Develop social skills
C. Be trusted and able to act → autonomously	← C. Trusting relationship
D. Acceptance by other kids →	D. Learn responsibility
E. Opportunities to socialize with guys	E. Develop positive, lifelong values

As we clarified the task, we realized that the question we needed to tackle was not "will she go out this Friday night with David?" but rather "what will our approach be to dating?" We wanted to resolve the issue in a way that would ensure that we would not need to address it again week after week. So we started to talk about the interests that each of us brought to the conversation, and we developed a list that looked something like Table 5.2. As we discussed the situation, each of our motivations became clear, and we soon realized that many of them were mutual, as indicated by the arrows that indicate that the "other" stakeholder shares the interest.

Then we started thinking about an approach that would allow us to address these needs. We started to generate some options, and came up with a list like the one in Table 5.3.

Once we thought we had a viable set of options that might address all the concerns, we began to evaluate the list and select the most intriguing possibilities. We evaluated it against the interests and the BATNA, the best alternative to a negotiated agreement for any of us. In this case, if we could not reach an agreement, we most likely would have simply refused to let her go out with "David." But we recognized that she would either comply with our edict, and resent us, or very possibly defy our order. Neither was a very attractive alternative for anyone, which increased everyone's motivation to reach a mutually acceptable outcome.

After using some of the tools and techniques that are described in Chapter 9, we developed a straw proposal that reflected our best thinking up to that point. We made no commitments at that stage, but developed a concept (like the one that is described in Table 5.4) that we could review together.

Table 5.3   Approach to Dating Options

1. Daughter tells in advance who will drive

2. Call home when plans change

3. No dating

4. Parent chaperones all dates

5. DMV background check on all drivers

6. Date only same age classmates

7. No restrictions

8. Pre-agreed upon destination

9. Parents meet prospective dates

10. Dates must be in town, unless special permission

11. Only double dating (until age 16½)

12. Midnight curfew

13. Agreement to talk about "undiscussables" (sex, drinking, etc.) on an ongoing basis

Our discussions continued until we had a plan that all of us could comfortably implement and that, incidentally, did include a date with David that Friday night. It also included a commitment to revisit our approach regularly as time went by to be certain that no one felt committed to anything with which they couldn't ultimately live. Surprisingly, this approach served us fairly well over many years and, although we had expected to have to modify it significantly, very little change was ever necessary.

SUMMARY

Our experience as parents has mirrored what we encounter in the workplace. A willingness to draw the circle around the whole team and to put the key interests and motivations ahead of the search for solution makes it possible to get the work done well and to create and maintain relationships that deliver great results over a long term.

Table 5.4   Approach to Dating Straw Design

1. Until further notice, all destinations will be pre-announced, and there will be a call home if plans need to be changed

2. Expectations that all "dates" will be introduced to at least one parent

3. Plans will also include information, and possible negotiation of transportation plans, including who drives

4. "No fault" rescue policy if problems occur

5. Dates must be in town, unless special permission

8. Only group dating (until age 16½)

9. Midnight curfew on Friday and Saturday nights

10. One date per week

11. Agreement to talk about "undiscussables" (sex, drinking, etc.) on an ongoing basis

These approaches and the processes that follow are designed to keep problem solvers working together mindfully to create coherence and successfully address conflict. That process begins in Chapter 6 with a discussion of how to align the group.

CHAPTER SIX

Aligning the Team

Several years ago I began working with a city director of public works whose department was plagued with infighting and competition between the divisions. He had analyzed the dynamics of the key stakeholders and determined that any efforts to address the situation would have the best chance of success if he personally led the discussions, and so he asked for some coaching on how to approach the task. He had little formal training in process skills, so we began working together to prepare him to lead a set of meetings designed to identify the barriers to a high performing team, and to allow participants to address some critical issues that were negatively impacting the ability of individuals and divisions to collaborate.

The greatest challenge in this undertaking was to help a strong leader, who was by his own admission process averse, to align the team members in a way that they were willing and able to work with each other on their common tasks. The director, like so many leaders with very full plates, was used to just jumping into problems and fixing them. He knew that he wanted something different for this group, and that he would need to take the time to ensure that participants had the ability and the desire to work together to address the problems themselves.

ADDRESSING THE WHOLE ORGANISM

The director understood that careful planning would be needed to move this group from discord to a place of generative engagement that would stick long after the boss had left the room. He soon discovered that the organizational task was more complex than simply calling a

81

Figure 6.1   The Dimensions of Problem Solving

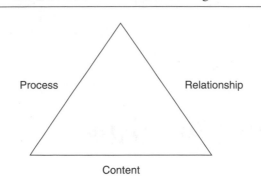

Process

Relationship

Content

meeting and starting to work on the content issues, which was his natural inclination, and is what most people do. There are three important dimensions, illustrated in Figure 6.1, that need to be considered when significant organizational issues are addressed. Each of these dimensions are factors at every stage of problem solving, so tools for each are included throughout the next four chapters.

The *content* describes the issues or the subject matter that stakeholders have come together to address. In the case of the public works department, some of the content they were tackling included communication, organization of the new corporation yard, equipment sharing, training, and project cleanup.

The *process* involves how a group will organize itself for a given task. Many groups use discussion and voting, or discussion and the boss deciding, as the default process tools in their meetings. There are certainly situations in which those tools may well be the most appropriate ones, but to paraphrase Abraham Maslow, "if your only tool is a hammer, then everything will look like a nail."

The next four chapters include a variety of possible process approaches, and it is critical that the approach for a meeting or an activity be compatible with the desired outcome. The public works director and his leadership staff were searching for some process tools that would cause the department members to understand each other's needs, own any results, and take on responsibility for implementing them. He also wanted them to experience some collaborative process tools that would intrigue them enough to want to apply them in other situations and to want to participate in problem solving process training.

The *relationship* of the participants is the third key dimension, and it is often the one that is most important and that we are least comfortable addressing. Often when there are significant problems there are also big issues dividing the parties, so the greatest barriers to an agreement are polarizing perceptions of resistance, fear, and mistrust. It is extremely difficult to reach agreements on content when there are undiscussable relationship issues dividing participants.

This was a very significant factor in the public works situation. The event planners identified a sizable list of relationship problems that were affecting the situation, including the following:

1. Old baggage/animosity

2. Loss of credibility by department members

3. Perceived lack of respect

4. Arguing, blame, and defensiveness

5. Personality conflicts

6. Perceptions of favoritism and double standards

7. Not being on the same page

8. Work groups not getting all the information

9. Withholding of information

10. Lack of trust

The director needed to plan the kind of learning to ensure that this old relationship baggage would not prevent them from being successful in their content issues. As a result he organized for the task in a way that safely surfaced these perceptions, and that eliminated the feelings of mistrust, disrespect, competition, and blame.

This chapter examines why leaders need to consider all three of these components as they align their teams in the first important stage of leading through collaboration.

THINKING ABOUT THE PROCESS—ORGANIZING THE TEAM

Creating a container for problem solving is very much like preparing the soil for planting. Lush garden growth is dependent on rich, well-nourished soil with all the conditions necessary for plants to thrive. Similarly, an environment in which organizational learning and problem solving can thrive must be structured accordingly. When participants in facilitation workshops are asked what such an environment looks like, they give a variety of different responses, including, for example:

- Participants feel relatively safe, equally valued, respected, and accountable—no power differential
- The physical setting is comfortable, neutral, distraction-free, and promotes engagement
- There is a commitment to an agenda, including shared outcomes, and time and schedule needs are respected
- Opportunities for personal connection are encouraged and created
- There is a commitment to the fundamental working relationship and keeping a Big Picture perspective
- There is a group record visible to all
- Honesty and openness abound
- Inquiry and advocacy are well balanced
- The atmosphere is open, reflective, creative, and celebrates "aha's"
- There is effective listening

All this means that a leader who is serious about creating coherence is thinking seriously from the very beginning of the problem solving process about how to arrange the team around all the components of the task. Participants can be organized physically and procedurally in a way that allows them to see the world through different lenses, as well as helping the group from the outset to stay on one page, rather than allowing them to polarize into competing perspectives. Let us consider each of these approaches—the physical and the procedural—as we think about the process elements of aligning the team.

Creating a Space—Organizing the Physical Logistics

Harrison Owen (1997), who has popularized the practice of *open space technology* in which large numbers of people in an organization come together in a self-organizing conference format, is meticulous about creating the space for his meetings. Although the meeting format is by definition "open," the environment is very thoughtfully conceived through the process of "creating and holding time and space." Owen understands that a meeting space cannot just be thrown together. The forum itself must be thoughtfully created with the right resources, seating, sight lines, and acoustics to ensure that the work of the meeting gets done well. Owen's "technology" is based on an understanding of how coherence principles can be effectively applied as it acknowledges that the space must be "held" in a way that the alignment that is needed for people to think together happens as quickly and effectively as possible. His own unique way of creating and holding the space involves setting up the physical environment well in advance and taking the time for intensive meditation in the meeting place early in the morning prior to the event (pp. 59–62).

Whereas Owen's methods of preparing may seem extreme to most of us, they are thoughtfully designed to create and maintain a level of coherence that will enable very large groups of people to think productively together. It is as important to think carefully about the venue for a meeting as it is for a wedding, a banquet, or a memorial service. Anyone faced with the task of planning a special function thinks about the kind of event and atmosphere that is desired, then puts together the elements that are needed to ensure that the goals are met. This means thinking about who is included, where the event is held, what size room will be needed, how to organize the seating, such as who sits where, and so on.

Remember from Figure 3.2 in Chapter 3 how important it is to organize the seating in a way that ensures that meeting participants are placed so that they see themselves as partners working together to focus on common goals. Seating is often in a horseshoe or a semicircle, with stakeholders well mixed, and everyone able to see and interact with each other, as well as the group record that hangs prominently at the front of the room. The space is generally free of distractions, and there is an ample supply of marking pens, flipcharts, easels, tape, and any other technologies or materials that are needed to support the meeting. This implies that there has been ample thought given to preparing the agenda so that planners will know what supplies will be necessary for an effective meeting.

In my own school district, our district level administrative team has systematized the use of a laptop computer and LCD projector to keep our group record. Support staff set up the equipment before each meeting, and team members take turns scribing for every item via the laptop. We moved to this logistical arrangement because, in order to strengthen communication, we have committed to distributing the meeting record to the management team, union leadership, the school board, and the county office of education as soon as possible after each meeting. This has also saved us a great deal of time editing transcripts, because everyone in attendance can verify instantly if the report is accurate. A flipchart, pens, and ample wall space are also available to facilitate thorny problem solving when necessary.

Thinking About Procedures—How Form Follows Function

Whereas the logistical organization of a meeting may be more consistent from session to session or topic to topic, the procedures that are used will vary depending on the goal. There is an old adage in the organization development world that "form should follow function," which essentially means that how you do something will depend on what you want to do. There are a wide variety of approaches that can be used to lead a group through a problem solving conversation, and the leaders of a group must collaborate to determine which structuring techniques are most useful for a given task. Different principles apply, depending on the purpose of the meeting. For example, very different approaches would be used if a meeting were intended to resolve a relationship problem, than if it were to evaluate a program, or set strategic direction. Several recent examples from my own organization will help to illustrate.

Formal Governance Meetings

When we have a board meeting, Robert's Rules of Order are applied, with motions, seconds, public hearings, and formal votes. A clerk keeps carefully prescribed minutes, which become a public record of the meeting, once they are transcribed as approved. These procedures ensure a high level of acceptance, accountability and fairness as it relates to the public's right to know about the official business being conducted on its behalf. The same format applies to other public meetings—city councils, planning commissions, special governmental committees, and so on.

Large Group Interventions

We recently held a community conference with about 200 people who assembled on a Saturday to work together to create shared meaning on the strategic priorities of the district. While no official business needed to be voted on that day, it was our purpose to get a broad level of involvement in the meeting, which was formally noticed as a board meeting because most of the trustees attended. So we organized participants into table groups, which were shuffled later in the day to provide fresh perspectives to participants, and we asked the groups to respond to a series of questions related to the future of the district. A structuring tool was used to collect the output on note cards under specific category headings, and the data was reviewed later by a subcommittee and refined into six strategic priorities with a variety of next steps implementation ideas. Careful planning went into the development of the procedures that were to be used, and it delivered the desired results. There were a variety of approaches that could have helped organize the event, many of which are summarized in *Large Group Interventions* by Alban and Bunker (1997), but the procedures in the facilitation plan needed to be developed with a thoughtful eye on our intended outcomes.

Group Problem Solving

A meeting in which participants gathered to begin shaping approaches and priorities for the school district budget provides a final example. In this instance, we used procedures that were introduced in Chapter 5 and will be more thoroughly explained at the end of this chapter and in Chapters 7 through 9. First we articulated the task for the day, which was to gain clarity on our budget priorities, and to illuminate the elements of the budget that needed to be addressed in negotiations with employee groups. We then charted the core interests that related to the task, generated options for areas that should be funded and possible areas that could be cut, and prioritized those lists so that we had a straw design to share

These tasks are basic elements in the problem solving process. Information on how to clarify the task is discussed later in this chapter, while identifying interests is discussed in Chapter 7. Chapter 8 provides techniques related to option generation, and Chapter 9 describes the straw design tool.

with the district budget action team, the employee groups, and the school board.

Force Field Analysis: The Swiss Army Knife of Process Tools

The force field analysis, developed by social psychologist Kurt Lewin (1938), is a time-honored process tool for problem analysis and planning. Its primary purpose is to identify the factors in the environment or situation impacting the ability of a group to realize its goal. It is particularly useful in surfacing the broad array of contributing factors that need to be addressed in order to resolve a given problem. A good way to understand how it works is to imagine a soccer or football field. The driving forces are represented by the offense, working to move the "ball" toward the goal line, and the restraining factors, like the defense, are hindering those efforts as they try to keep the ball away from the goal line. Enhancing the offense and diminishing the defense will increase the chances of reaching the goal. The Force Field tool can be applied with equal usefulness to process, content, and relationship problems. These are the basic steps:

Tools and Techniques

1. Draw a T-chart (see Figure 6.2).

2. Define the current "As Is" situation as thoughtfully and thoroughly as possible. There should be clarity on what is the status quo and why a change is desirable.

3. Define the desired condition or goal to be reached. Make the goal statement as specific and detailed as possible. Quantify where appropriate.

4. Identify both the driving and restraining forces that operate to produce the current situation. Focus on forces that are currently at work.

> *Driving forces:*   Behaviors, situations, and circumstances that are helping the group toward its desired condition or goal.
>
> *Restraining forces:*   Behaviors, situations, and circumstances that impede or hinder the group's ability to reach its desired condition or goal.

5. Assess the relative strength of the factors on both lists. Use a number scale or a high/medium/low impact rating.

6. Using this evaluation, determine whether any of the factors identified need further research in order to be fully understood.

7. If you are using the force field analysis for planning purposes, identify which factors should receive the most attention. The objective is to strengthen the driving forces and weaken the effect of the restraining forces in order to shift the equilibrium in the direction of the desired condition. Changing a restraining force into a driving force is a powerful strategy.

   Look at the restraining forces:
   - Which will be hardest to address?
   - Which would be easiest?
   - How long and what resources would it take?

   Look at the driving forces:
   - Could any be made more effective?
   - Could any be used in other ways?
   - Could other helping forces be added?

8. Isolate the factors to be addressed and, using problem-solving techniques, develop action plans accordingly.

9. Implement the action plans and schedule reflection for the purpose of monitoring and improving the changes.

10. The force field can also be used to generate a list of counterpart helping behaviors, based on what is not working. This can be a simple and effective way to norm a group.

THINKING ABOUT THE CONTENT—ARTICULATING THE TASK

A group that is well aligned must be very clear about the content to be addressed, as well as the processes to be followed. The problems that can result from an inadequate sense of the task at hand is illustrated by an experience I had with a school district group that was negotiating the start times for schools based on some recent changes

Figure 6.2   Sample Use of the Force Field Analysis

As Is: Dysfunctional and unproductive meetings
Goal: Consistently effective meetings

Driving Forces ⟶	Restraining Forces ⟵
Mixed seating	Poor framing of problem (defining/clarifying) *High
Clear agenda	Blame, accusatory language, and personal attacks
Quiet meeting room	No explicit ground rules *High
Starting and ending on time	Not listening *Medium
Regularly scheduled meetings	Not stating what is heard—lots of defending
Taking turns running the meeting	Inadequate prior preparation and lack of process planning *High
	Facilitator too attached to content (not neutral enough) *Medium

to the state regulations. As we got started, they initially identified two issues that needed to be addressed:

1. When will students start school each day based on state mandated changes?

2. When will teachers at each school begin their professional workday?

As we told the story, some frustration emerged based on conflicting mental models of the problem. We discovered that each participant in the discussion had a very different perspective on the task based on the participant's role, the particular school where each worked, and the number of years each had worked in the district. The topic was a hot

Figure 6.3   Describe What You See

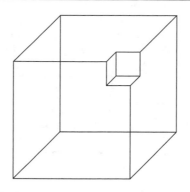

one because everyone's experience of the issue was so widely varied. It became apparent from the nature of the discussion that we needed to slow down the conversation to make sure that we had a common understanding of the data that surrounded the issue.

Telling the Story

It is the very nature of a group that each of its members will see the world differently based on unique lenses of culture, knowledge, and experience. Test this assumption by examining Figure 6.3 with someone else, and describe to each other what you see.

Though there are multiple ways of experiencing a figure as concrete as this one, we tend to get locked into our own comfortable way of seeing things. Once our eyes have been "tuned" to the perspective of others, it even tends to change the certainty with which we view our own original perspectives. People often have difficulty seeing the figure the "old" way once they have seen one of the alternate perspectives. Incidentally, there are at least five or six different ways of seeing this cube, so keep going if you have stopped at two!

There is a natural tendency for individuals to see and advocate for their own, comfortable perspectives, as opposed to those advanced by others, so we become sucked into conflict, even before we have taken the time to understand the differences in those points of view. Chris Argyris (1993, 2000) is credited with developing the *ladder of*

Figure 6.4   The Ladder of Inference

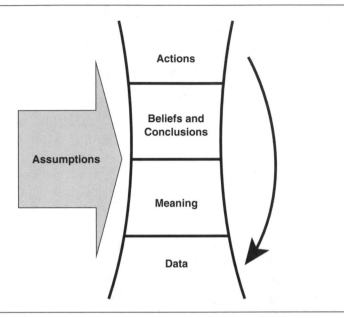

inference (Figure 6.4) to depict the nature of this conflict. We are constantly bombarded with data and in order to survive, we sort it into a recognizable order based on the way we experience the world. We climb the ladder of inference based on the way each of us processes the data we experience, and we often fail to check out what we assume to be true, or to seek to understand the perspective of others. When there is conflict, or a need to work with others to resolve problems, we must climb down our ladders to the point that we can build shared meaning together, so that we at least understand the situation from all points of view.

Often this means going all the way down to the data to ensure that everyone is forming a database of the same information. What we discovered in our meeting to address school start times is that there were some widely varied implementations at each of the schools, even though each of them was supposed to be implementing the same contract provisions. Some teachers were allowed to begin school 20 minutes later than others who were supposed to be working the same student schedule, and some principals found that they had been holding teachers accountable to standards of which others were either unaware, or were ignoring completely.

Going Back to the Data

Successful problem solving often involves naming and understanding the facts and the data that lie at the bottom of the stakeholders' respective ladders of inference. Data needs will vary widely depending on the issue, but can include some of the following:

- A history of the problem
- Relevant quantitative information including budget data and statistical information such as incidence, frequency, and distribution of problem characteristics
- Analysis of practices and procedures
- Data concerning opinions and attitudes
- Feelings and impacts on people's lives

Often the data is most effectively gathered by convening the key stakeholders to tell their stories. In other instances, plans must be made for group members to gather the desired data. Make sure that when the research needs have been identified, there are clear assignments of responsibility and timelines for when work is expected to be completed and available for the group. This can be done at any time, but it is best if data

Tools and Techniques

needs are identified and addressed as early as possible, especially if the needed information is complex and the gathering will be time consuming (as in the case of a salary or job classification study). It is highly unlikely that a successful result can be achieved without creating coherence around the data.

Defining the Task

As the origins of the problem were traced, the group discovered that no one in the room had been around when the variances started occurring, so a senior staff member was summoned who could tell the rest of the story. The team quickly realized that 7 years earlier, changes had been made to the afternoon recess that had caused different schools to implement widely varying teacher schedules. By the time the inquiry had ended, the problem solvers realized the most critical issue had not even been articulated:

"How will we address the inconsistencies in teacher start time and workday implementations across the district?"

Once they had a common definition of the task, the appropriate solution fell into place with remarkable speed. The key to successfully understanding the problem involved sharing the data that had caused the individuals to see the world so differently. This shared understanding, when combined with the interests that each of the parties brought to the discussion, led them like a red carpet to the option that met everyone's needs acceptably, which involved development of a process to ensure greater consistency in instructional hours throughout the district. A group that is well aligned to solve difficult problems together must be working off the same page when it comes to the issues or questions they are striving to resolve.

> *See Chapter 7 for more about interests and the ladder of inference, and Chapter 8 for additional information on options.*

Getting Everyone on the Same Page

One of the challenges in defining the task, is to articulate the group's charge in a way that frames the issues so all participants can understand the task at hand, and can focus on the common goal that it represents. The task clarifies what needs to be addressed in the problem solving or negotiations and serves the function of setting the agenda for the meeting. The distinguishing characteristics for defining the task are listed in Table 6.1. A well-defined task will be free of blame and bias, and will be so acceptable to the group that everyone can nod their heads in agreement that, "if we can pull this off we will have done great work."

> *Tools and Techniques*

We knew in our school schedule meetings that it could be a tall order getting the group on the same page, but we also knew how important it would be to our ultimate success to find a way to align the group early on in the process so they saw themselves as members of one team focused on a common task, rather than as opponents or adversaries. The process of defining the task provided the perfect opportunity for that alignment, so the group set to work telling the story and listening for the common ground that would get them all on the same page.

Table 6.1   Distinguishing Characteristics for a Well-Articulated Task

1. It can often be expressed as an open-ended question(s) followed by additional issues/topics to be covered in the group's inquiry, search, or discussion.

2. It sets the direction of the inquiry.

3. It should be solvable.

4. It is neutrally stated without bias, defensiveness, or blame.

5. It unifies the diverse parties to focus on common goals.

6. It is considered to be a working definition of the task. It may change once there is a more thorough understanding of the circumstances.

7. Good task/problem definitions:
   ❑ Are short—try less than 20 words
   ❑ May pose a question (How shall we. . .? What can we do about . . . . ?)
   ❑ May be quantified, measurable, or specific
   ❑ Focus on current conflict, issues or problems
   ❑ Do not incorporate a cause – (i.e., state what needs to be addressed, not why it needs to be addressed)
   ❑ Do not incorporate a solution – (i.e., state what needs to be addressed, not what must be done to cure it)

Sometimes we make that process more difficult than it really needs to be. Table 6.2 shows four different approaches to defining the undertaking for a school district task force formed when parents reacted negatively to a district plan to reduce busing. The key to aligning the group on one page at this early stage of engagement is finding a way to frame the task neutrally without blame or bias.

It is not unusual to see a group laboring to construct a *problem statement* that inclusively reflects everyone's perspective. This "kitchen sink approach" can certainly be very helpful to the group in achieving coherence if successfully crafted. But the time and effort required to produce such a comprehensive statement might be more fruitfully invested in finding an actual solution. My own bias is that the unadorned, open-ended question reflected in the *simple approach* is easy to do and achieves the primary goal of aligning all the participants around a common task. The bulleted topics become the agenda items under the umbrella statement, and they represent the

Table 6.2   Four Approaches to Defining the Task

The Blameful Approach	What can we do about the district's inept blunders around the proposed transportation cuts?
The Biased Approach	How can we implement the transportation cuts as proposed?
The Kitchen Sink Approach	How can we ensure the safe, economical, and efficient transportation of our students to their schools at the beginning and end of the school day in a way that produces a positive relationship between parents and district officials, and that ensures excellent achievement in the students' academic endeavors as well as resolving parent concerns about supervision and child care?
A Simple Approach	What will we do about our transportation problem? • Safety • Budget • Supervision and child care • Communications

issues that must be addressed for the work to be completed success-fully. The work on transportation could not have been finished for one group or another until *both* the safety *and* the budget issues had been acceptably addressed.

Listening for the "Both/And"

The ear can be tuned to hear the discussion in a way that allows the task to emerge out of the storytelling. Everyone needs at least a brief opportunity to initially explain their view of the situation (as in the cube in Figure 6.3), including their experiences with the problem. The

Tools and Techniques

initial telling of the story will naturally and spontaneously include interests and options, and leaders will need to become skilled at cap-turing the data in the appropriate list. When it feels that everyone has been heard, or the conversation is becoming repetitive, then it is time to attempt to clarify the task.

In particularly thorny situations, it can really help to include per-spectives in the task statement, because they can be helpful in enlist-ing commitment to a shared enterprise. An individual is far more likely to buy into a problem solving process that recognizes, and promises to address, his or her core needs. An easy way to frame the seemingly competing perspectives is to name the polarization in the group and attempt to reprogram the divisiveness in a way that puts everyone on the same page. It might sound something like this, "So it's clear that the parents who are here have a primary concern for the safety of their children. While the district seems to share that interest, there is also a need to consider budgetary constraints as well. So perhaps our task is to find a transportation solution that addresses both the safety *and* the financial interests."

The most important community-building needs get addressed in this way. Each party is able to commit to the problem solving because each feels heard and sees its core interests reflected in the task. Whereas nothing guarantees an acceptable result at the other end, each sees some tangible hope that the promised search might produce a result that addresses the highest priority interests.

Pointers for Defining the Task

1. Check the validity of the problem statement once you have a good understanding of the story. Ask:
   - Does the data validate the task/problem as it has been defined?
   - Does the task definition appropriately reflect that circumstance?

   Tools and Techniques

   - Now that we understand the problem, is it solvable? Do we still want to solve it?

2. Revise the task/problem definition if necessary.

THINKING ABOUT THE
RELATIONSHIP—ALIGNING THE TEAM

The discussion in Chapter 3 made the case for the need to align the behavior of group members if they are to be able to move to generative engagement. I have discovered over many years that I can bank on the "politeness" response occurring when groups assemble and organize, at least momentarily, in the first quadrant (*compliance*) of Figure 3.4. Even the most combative of groups generally comes together politely—at least for a while—as group members check out the situation and find their bearings. Participants often expect the best at the beginning, and are open to suggestions that might help them organize themselves as positively as possible. I remember one woman entering the room I had prepared for a neighborhood meeting on affordable housing and inspecting the draft ground rules that had been posted. When she got to "attack problems not people" she turned to me and asked, "Wow, what have they told you about us?"

Without a specific agreement on how people should act, they will behave according to habit, and those behaviors could undermine the coherence that the leader is trying to create. Another community group included a number of rancorous individuals with a notorious reputation for never successfully completing a full meeting together without bitter interpersonal exchanges that left someone storming away in anger. The politeness of the first meeting of the newly convened group was utilized to develop behavioral expectations, and those guidelines kept the group working comfortably, civilly, and effectively together over the five meetings and almost 15 hours that they spent together.

Addressing Relationship Problems

While the *norming* processes described below help to keep relationships healthy and aligned, groups are often in conflict because of interpersonal relationship problems. I was asked a number of years ago to mediate a labor relationship that had been at an impasse for months in a salary negotiation. The dispute involved a school district and the bargaining unit that represented drivers, custodians, food service workers, and other blue-collar, noncertificated employees. I had learned in the assessment process leading up to the session that relationships were somewhat toxic, and that bargaining to that point had been characterized by a certain degree of adversarialism. I also learned that there were no agreements in place that prohibited disrespectful or adversarial behavior. As the process got started that day we clarified behavioral ground rules, and then began working on the content of the meeting. Relationships were guarded and polite, consistent with quadrant one of Figure 3.4. I was a new participant who had been added to the equation and at least for a while, everyone was on his or her best behavior.

But as they got used to me, they began to behave much more comfortably and normally, and an adversarial streak began to show itself as might be expected of a group in discord as described in quadrant two of Figure 3.4. One woman in particular (a leader of the union bargaining team) seemed to become increasingly irritable and angry around comments from members of the management team. Finally, in one particular moment of exasperation, she verbally attacked the character and integrity of the organization's business manager, who also happened to be the chair of the management bargaining team. The group sat silently for a moment and the manager who had been attacked seemed to be contemplating the appropriate response.

I intervened in the content of the meeting by asking for a process check to talk about what had just happened. I specifically named the attacking behavior that had caused the group to stop in its tracks and my interests related to the incident by identifying process, content, and relationship concerns that came up for me. "Isabel, it really felt to me like you were lashing out at Richard just then, and it raised concerns for me on three different levels. First it was a clear violation of our process ground rules in which we committed to attack problems not people. Second, it is preventing us from dealing with the important content issues we came here to address in the negotiations process. And finally, when your comment comes out like an attack, I believe that it makes Richard withdraw from the conversation, and denies all of us access to the wisdom and important insight that you are bringing to our discussion and that lie beneath your words."

Most interestingly, "Isabel's" behavior changed immediately once her behavior was named and there was acknowledgment of the negative impact on the group's work, and how her adversarialism was undermining her own ability to advocate her needs effectively with Richard and the rest of the management team. The adversarial behavior not only disappeared immediately, but the group reached agreement on their entire contract within the next hour. They were at an impasse not because they were at odds on the substance of their negotiations, but because relationship issues were impeding their ability or their willingness to reach an agreement.

Unpack the Baggage

It is sometimes very useful, when there are relationship issues impacting a group's ability to work together on the content, to take some time after telling the story to allow apparent antagonists to share what they have learned to be the other party's perspective on the situation. All too often, people come to a dispute convinced that the others don't appreciate or understand their perspective. And so, after telling the story, it can be very helpful to have the group summarize without attacking or blame, how the other party sees it. Invariably this process will surface the critical relationship issues, and it will often eliminate the kind of behavior that was undermining "Isabel," "Richard," and the team described above.

Tools and Techniques

Taking Time for the Relationship

A group that is striving to reach coherence must take as much time as is needed to ensure that relationships are aligned well enough to allow the group's work to be completed. Small rubs in relationships will often lead to much larger breakdowns in content. So despite our eagerness to get our substantive work done, we need to slow down enough to talk about how things are going in the relationships. Leaders must be comfortable setting ground rules that will allow participants the comfort that they need to talk honestly about the problems that are part of their working interactions.

The Force Field Analysis tool described earlier in this chapter is an excellent device for allowing group members to discuss their relationships rationally and comfortably. With rigorous ground rules in place (as described later in this chapter) groups can have open and comfortable conversations by talking about the factors that are promoting excellent working relationships, and those that get in the way. It is sometimes helpful to divide participants into small groups to protect anyone who might feel fearful of speaking out to the whole team. Generating and enforcing norms or ground rules can correct problematic behaviors or dynamics that are identified. Prudent leaders will not wait for their groups to become dysfunctional before introducing these conversations, but rather will schedule regular relationship "tune-ups" as preventative maintenance for their team's coherence.

Tools and Techniques

Understanding Norms

A critical aspect of attending to the relationships is aligning behavior so that individuals are acting in ways that ensure that the processes that are used and the relationships that are created are likely to deliver the desired content outcomes. Certain situations will require individuals to behave and interact differently than others. For example, I described in Chapter 5 the organizations that are working to create collaborative labor-management teams to resolve problems and do some strategic decision making. When those organizations are fire departments, the behavior in those meetings looks very different than it does when a team of firefighters responds to a call. While consultation and collaboration are still factors, the emergency nature of the call requires a set of command and control behaviors that would generally not be appropriate in a labor management team meeting.

This alignment between behavior and outcome can be achieved through the creation of norms, which are a set of behavioral expectations considered to be appropriate by the members of a group or organization. The reason a group adopts norms is to ensure that they are *explicitly* identifying the behavior that is expected to support the vision, values, and core needs of the organization.

However, sometimes the group adopts these norms *implicitly* in the form of unspoken agreements that govern the way a group operates. These unspoken agreements may not even be an accurate reflection of the actual behaviors that the members of the group prefer. For example, most people say they value their time and that they want meetings to start and end on time. But if the issue has not been formally or consciously addressed, new participants may begin to notice an organizational habit that all meetings start 10 minutes late. Realizing that nothing will happen right away, participants use the 10 minutes to make another phone call or check e-mail, and they do not even begin to arrive until the "traditional" 10 minutes have passed, and so the habit is perpetuated.

Sometimes implicit norming can be very positive. Soon after the popularization of automated teller machines (ATMs), I began to observe that patrons waiting in line to use the machines would queue up across the sidewalk, or some respectful distance away in order to provide the current user with appropriate privacy. I do not recall an instruction book, sign, or communication from the bank suggesting how people should line up for ATMs. The respectful behavior just seemed to reflect a natural human self-organization that created instant coherence on how to do it.

However, implicit norms are often problematic. Table 6.3 lists examples of other implicit norms that may cause a group to

Table 6.3   Examples of Counterproductive Implicit Norms

1. Start meetings 10 minutes late

2. Use foul language

3. The rumor mill is a viable place to collect data

4. Never question the boss

5. It is okay to attack people

6. Hurtful humor is welcome

7. Answer your cell phone anytime. It is a good indication of how important you are

inadvertently perpetuate undesirable behaviors in the culture. It is important to clarify that no one sits down to consciously mandate these behaviors. They are the result of innate habits that simply emerge when people interact together naturally, and they are the behaviors that are most likely to lead to relationship conflicts.

Using the Negative to Create the Positive

Generally norms are created to specifically address negative interactions that are impeding group effectiveness. They commonly cannot be transferred from one group to another, unless those two groups are experiencing similar organizational dynamics. In this sense, groups often need to "reinvent the wheel" when it comes to relationship guidelines.

An easy way to norm a group is to dialogue about the kinds of behavior that is hindering the group from performing effectively together. By using the Force Field Analysis tool described earlier in the chapter, the list of hindrances will suggest helpful behaviors that, if implemented, would improve the dynamics of the situation.

Tools and Techniques

For example, the expectations listed in Table 6.4 were drafted by one school district after a series of conversations revealed a set of behaviors that were impeding the ability of the group to work together effectively. This is the same district described in Chapter 3, which began its relationship work with a school board retreat. These

Table 6.4   Are We Clear on How We Do Business Together?

1. We will treat each other with courtesy and respect, modeling good learning behavior.

2. We will strive to meet deadlines and arrive on time, prepared to do our work.

3. We will strive to avoid surprising each other whenever possible.

4. When we question each other's motives or when we disagree with something that is occurring, we will initiate a constructive discussion to resolve the matter.

5. We will strive to not make assumptions about each other's motivations.

6. We will strive to be strategic and goal driven in our work.

7. We will strive to check for understanding whenever possible.

norms were modified for the whole district to use based on a larger list that was extracted from the unproductive behaviors identified earlier by the school board at their retreat. So many of the hindering behaviors of the school board also applied to general interactions within the district that the whole community embraced this list.

When I join a group for the first time I make an effort whenever possible to check on the expectations for how people work together in the group. If there are none, I try to help establish them. Even if the group is coming together for a limited period of time, I like to encourage creating a set of ground rules that will clarify how participants expect to interact in that time frame. Our family has even seen the value of norming ourselves on occasion when our grown daughters return to visit or when we travel together. Each of us has expectations of what we want it to look like, and each of us has needs and commitments that will impact the others and our various expectations of how we will spend time together. If we don't clarify those expectations early on, we inevitably experience conflict based on those differing expectations that we bring to the situation.

Ground Rules Made Easy

Ground rules are a very simple set of norms that are needed to ensure that meetings go well. However brief the projected life span of a newly forming group, perhaps the most important thing it can do to vault toward generative problem solving is to put ground rules in place that ensure that meetings stay on track and that there are commitments to interpersonal behavior consistent with the goals and

the vision of participants. Failure to do so permits dynamics to occur that can threaten the common enterprise. The following easy steps are designed to ensure that ground rules are developed efficiently and painlessly. In most cases it can be accomplished in 10 minutes or less, an investment well worth the potential return.

Tools and Techniques

1. Clarify the Purpose of Ground Rules

I have found over time that people act relatively rationally when they are given the reasons for behaving in a certain way. Stated simply, ground rules serve to keep a group mindful of the kinds of behavior that will allow a group to work together effectively. They are intended as commitments about what behavior should look like and as a means for group members to hold each other accountable to those guidelines.

2. The Group Leader/Facilitator Begins by Listing Two or Three Ground Rules

These can be nonnegotiable, but they also need to be reasonable rules that rational participants are likely to accept. They should also include, if needed, any explanation about why they are being suggested. These might include the following:

- Attack problems not people
- One person talks at a time—avoid side conversations
- Check out what you assume to be true
- No commitment will be assumed unless stated

I actually did experience a situation once when a member of the group resisted the "attack problems not people" ground rule on the basis that he wanted to attack the city officials for allowing a situation to unfold in a way that he did not accept. We acknowledged his perspective but indicated that, if the rest of the group accepted the rule, then it would apply to everyone. Hearing his perspective acknowledged and being given permission to describe the behavior that bothered him without making accusations or assumptions about intent, he accepted and followed the rule.

3. Invite the Group to Propose Additional Ground Rules

Ask the group for ground rules that they feel might support the interests of effective and orderly problem solving meetings. Collect them first as a brainstormed list without criticism or discussion. Explain to participants that they will have an opportunity in a few minutes to critique and modify the list. Stress that even the finished product will stand as a working draft, and can be modified and improved as the need appears.

4. Invite Comments and Discussion

"Are there any items on the list with which anyone might have difficulty agreeing?" When an item is identified, ask the participant what interests lie behind the objection, and how the item can be improved. Include an invitation for group members to work together off the common list and help the group to find ways of addressing the interests expressed. It is not unusual to find controversy in the ground rule discussion, but simple wording changes will often resolve the concerns. "Maintain confidentiality" might be intended to encourage honesty and candor, but it can conflict with the interest of team members to keep constituents well informed. "Honor a context of confidentiality and discuss in advance what will be reported to constituents" might meet all interests acceptably.

Whenever a participant in a large community gathering suggests that "all beepers and cell phones should be turned off," it is often met with dismay if others are sacrificing to attend the meeting and need to stay in touch with their offices or their families. When probed, the author of the suggestion invariably indicates a desire to minimize interruptions, and so a rule can be crafted with an expectation that ringers will be turned to silent mode, and any necessary distractions will immediately be taken out of the room.

5. Propose Closure When There Is No More Input, or When Major Concerns Seem to Have Been Addressed

When there is a sense that the group is ready to move on, ask for consensus, including a signal (for example thumbs up, sideways, or down) indicating whether group members can live with the rules. Anyone failing to indicate a preference should be pushed for a sign of acceptance or disagreement and any dissenting signals should be addressed. Ownership of the process rules is important enough to the group's ultimate ability to create coherence that discussions should continue until all participants can at least live with the final product.

See Chapter 9 to learn more about working with consensus, including signaling techniques.

6. Publish the Completed Rules and Establish Process Mechanisms for Ensuring They Are Enforced

Once rules have been established, make them visible, distribute them to new participants, and encourage everyone to assist the facilitator in monitoring and enforcing them. Facilitators should also check regularly that the rules are being followed and that they are modified accordingly as the needs of the group change.

SUMMARY

Aligning the team for effective problem solving involves attention to process, content, and relationship. Leaders should give thoughtful attention to *how* to proceed, to telling the story and clarifying the issues to be addressed, and to taking care to ensure that the people in the room have been aligned so that relationships are healthy and intact for effective problem solving. With the team well aligned, attention can be given to addressing the substantive content work of the group, including understanding the interests that are truly most important in the problem solving process. This process will be addressed in Chapter 7.

CHAPTER SEVEN

Focusing on the Vision

A city official was called out to work with a resident who was objecting to a new system of fire hydrants that were being installed on her street. A hydrant was scheduled for installation in front of her home, and, objecting to how unsightly the large and offensive looking hydrant would seem in her front yard, she made it clear that she wanted it moved to someone else's house. As the city representative explored the problem with the resident, it became clear that changing the appearance of the hydrant or its conspicuous location would not satisfy the resident.

He kept probing during the conversation to see if he could discover how best to help her address the situation. What he was eventually surprised to learn was that her real concern was not with the appearance of the hydrant, but with parking. The members of her family owned several cars, and the installation of the hydrant would likely include a no-parking zone, which would reduce the amount of available parking in front of their home. Once her real motivation had been discovered, the city representative could set to work helping her to address the underlying problem, which was not aesthetics but parking availability.

Similarly, schoolteachers and administrators interact on a daily basis with parents and students who are dissatisfied with the way things are, and who represent their concerns in a way that may not reveal the true reason behind the complaint. There is an old saying that knowledge is power, and so the use of interests is probably as powerful a tool as there is in gaining the understanding that facilitates creating coherence in groups. As we have seen, we all tend to approach the world with our own unique perspectives, and a deep understanding of the relevant interests involved gives us a huge amount of insight into what kinds of approaches will be needed to reach lasting agreement. Once I accept the fact that my own needs are more easily met if I can help you to meet yours (and thus eliminate any of your resistance that may be impeding my goals), then your interests gain great importance for me. The citizen who received help in finding a solution to her parking problem no longer presented an obstacle to the city's task of installing new fire hydrants, and so their work could proceed. So long as they were talking about the appearance of the hydrants, they were hopelessly deadlocked.

It's one thing to understand that identifying interests is important, and another to be able to use them as a powerful coherence tool. The basic concept is simple enough that it can generally be understood on the first explanation. Yet the ability to hear interests when positions are expressed, and to harness their potency to produce elegant agreements is a subtle and nuanced art that can take years of mindful practice to master. This chapter is intended to be the user guide for that practice.

CULTIVATING THE POWER OF INQUIRY

The citizen who was trying to get the city to move the planned hydrant away from her home was operating from a position, which is a fixed perspective of the world that generally includes a predetermined commitment to a course of action that is intended to resolve the situation at hand. She did what we all do, which is to mentally and emotionally climb our ladder of inference that was described in Figure 6.4. She observed a situation, formed an opinion about that situation based on the assumptions, meaning, and beliefs it conjured for her, and ultimately took action from that worldview by calling the city to complain and by demanding that the hydrant be moved away from her home.

Our own community is currently nearing completion of a freeway overpass that had been in planning for years, and that had been the subject of much debate and opposition over time. Many people opposed the project altogether because of a belief that the benefits of the overpass could never outweigh the inconveniences and frustrations of the long traffic delays they expected during the construction period. We even heard stories of people selling their homes and moving to the other side of town in order to avoid the impending mess. Imagine everyone's surprise to discover that the detours and systems that were created in order to address the traffic concerns were so effective that traffic moved far more efficiently during construction than it did before the renovation process had started.

These improvements did not happen by chance. The project planners listened to the concerns of citizens and designed a construction and detour system that would address those concerns. The solutions that they ultimately implemented addressed the interests that were raised, and as a result the whole community was happy with what many had expected to be a disastrous situation. In both the overpass and fire hydrant examples, rather than becoming paralyzed by the opposition they were encountering, savvy problem solvers were able to utilize the positional information that their stakeholders were providing to produce a result that met everyone's needs more effectively.

The Mindful Search for Understanding

There is probably a rationality gap separating behavior that focuses on positions versus interests. On the one hand there is a rigid adherence to traditional or habit-based perspectives, and on the other there is a conscious effort to understand the motivations that must be satisfied to produce effective outcomes. These differences are illustrated in Table 7.1, and they mirror the open and closed orientation that was discussed in Chapter 2. Coherence becomes possible when the parties are authentically engaged in a joint search for solutions, rather than imposing favorite solutions on each other. The heart of that search is an investigation into the interests, or the underlying motivations that are driving each of the parties.

I like to characterize the approach that is represented on the left hand column of Table 7.1 as an inquiry approach to problem solving because it most accurately conveys the proactive nature of the process. A careful examination of the two columns suggests that the quality of the inquiry established in a problem-solving relationship will be determined by the attitudes and intent that the parties bring to the working enterprise. Mindfully striving to understand underlying motivations can significantly improve the effectiveness of communication and

Table 7.1   Comparing Inquiry and Positionalism

Inquiry	Positionalism
1. Is based on mindfulness, and is useful in any approach to negotiation	1. Is based on habits—everyone has the tendency to be positional
2. Involves becoming vulnerable and opening things up in an effort to see things "their way"	2. Tends to include a fixed, self-protective, or closed perspective and is generally focused on seeing things "my way"
3. Provides mechanisms for inclusion and connectedness, keeping the parties working together on the same page	3. Is characterized by "separateness" (worrying primarily about my own perspective and meeting my own needs)
4. A joint search for solutions, focused on possibilities, not limitations	4. Knowing the best solution, with a focus on implementation not exploration
5. Encourages learning, combined with intent to end up seeing the world differently	5. Promotes performing, with a view toward looking good
6. Supports an effort to inspire joint commitment to a common cause, and to meet everyone's needs effectively	6. Involves striving to win via unilateral control over self and others
7. Involves taking responsibility for solving problems	7. Involves assigning blame for causing problems

problem solving, and enable a group to maintain a team-oriented search for solutions that meet everyone's needs acceptably.

INTERESTS: THE HEART OF THE SEARCH FOR SOLUTIONS

This joint search for solutions requires problem solvers to fashion agreements that acceptably address the needs of each of the stakeholders. Mary Parker Follett (1940) dubbed this process *integration*, for it requires an outcome that integrates diverse needs into one comprehensive approach. Chapter 8 focuses on the search for integrative solutions, but before moving to that phase of the process, it is critical to develop a deep understanding of what is truly motivating participants. Table 7.2 describes the distinguishing characteristics of an interest.

Table 7.2   Distinguishing Characteristics of an Interest

1. An interest can usually be satisfied in many different ways.

2. If it sounds like a reason or motivation, it is probably an interest.

   If it sounds like a specific or favorite solution, it is probably a position, not an interest. Beware of positions disguised as interests. ("I need . . . .")

3. An interest answers the question "why is that important to you?" at a fundamental level, so deep inquiry is often required to discover those core motivations.

4. The interests are the criteria against which a solution will be measured to determine its acceptability.

The key difference between an interest and a position is that an interest can be satisfied in a number of different ways, one of which might be the favorite solution that is being promoted by one or more of the parties involved. Consider this example, which we see often in labor negotiations. The issue concerns who is expected to "stand by" for call-back duty to address emergency maintenance problems at night, or in the evenings when maintenance staff are not scheduled for duty. An employee serving standby is often paid a stipend to carry a pager, and is generally obligated to return when paged to repair the problem, often at a designated overtime rate. In this particular organization, the union and management teams were in conflict because it was the union's position that standby coverage should be voluntary, while management pressed for mandatory service. They faced the typical winner/loser dilemma when they debated whose favorite solution was best. They were debating an either/or— it will either be mandatory or voluntary—so their negotiations were stalemated.

Inquiry and the Search for Solutions

The only way out of the impasse was to go to *inquiry* together to discover the reasons behind each of their positions. Both sides need to be willing to suspend their positional behavior to

> *Tools and Techniques: The arrows in Figure 7.1 reflect a facilitation technique designed to show graphically the mutual interests that are at work.*

Figure 7.1   Interests

Union		Management
A. Minimize wear and tear on employees	→	A. 24/7 coverage
B. Fairness	→ ←	B. Cost effectiveness
C. Sensitivity to differences in living circumstances		C. Timely and high quality response to repairs

discover common ground that might lead to a more satisfactory conclusion. Those reasons are listed in Figure 7.1.

Remember from our discussions in Part I of this book that problem solving is a process of discovery. *Inquiry* in this sense reflects a search for information, or an investigation into the underlying facts and perspectives related to the situation at hand. Moving to inquiry at this stage does not mean that any of the participants ultimately give up the right to revert to positionalism, but rather that they agree to suspend their innate inclination to go to fight-or-flight behavior. This is a critical step in any case, but especially helpful when we run into positions because there are almost always rational motivations that are causing people to advocate a certain solution.

Staying Both Firm and Flexible

Once we learn how to be firm in articulating and identifying the nature of our interests, while remaining flexible about how those needs get met, it becomes possible to use our new understanding as a litmus test to determine if we are successfully moving past positions. The manager who had been advocating for a mandatory standby rotation was asked, "If we can find a way to ensure complete coverage and a high quality response at no significant increase in cost, could you live with any solution that got us there?" The answer after some thought was "yes," so they all knew that they had successfully moved past the position.

Similarly, when the union was asked why a voluntary system was so important, the problem solvers learned that the increasing cost of housing in the area was causing employees to live further and further away. This made it less attractive to return to duty for the 2 hours of minimum overtime that was earned when employees were called back for a 15 minute repair. They acknowledged that, whereas the preferred solution was a voluntary standby program, any solution might be acceptable if it felt fair, addressed the need to honor differences in living situations, and minimized wear and tear on employees.

The search was on. Any solution would be acceptable so long as it met the identified needs, and suddenly the potential list of ideas was expanded from the original two to a much longer list of possibilities. Those possibilities included raising the rate that was paid for doing standby coverage, contracting out coverage to a private firm, paying a higher overtime rate for callbacks, increasing the minimum number of hours for each callback, and varying the rotation schedule in a number of ways. The idea of contracting out led to the notion that they could contract in by allowing the employees who wanted to do the work to form an internal group who would take responsibility for ensuring that the work got done well. This was not acceptable to management because of concerns that there would not be enough volunteers to ensure that they could meet their interest in avoiding gaps in coverage. So the concept was expanded to include a provision that management could monitor the coverage, and if at any point the standby team was not able to ensure full coverage, the mandatory system would be restored. With this addition, all the stakeholders felt that their needs had been addressed, and the issue was resolved.

Reframing Positions to Interests

Every position has an interest behind it, and an ability to apprehend those motivations quickly and efficiently during interpersonal interactions is a powerful platform for thinking and communicating effectively with others. Learning to understand people by gazing through the window of their motivations provides an effective lens for examining and understanding their perspectives.

People are often attracted to books and workshops on problem solving because they hope that they will acquire skills and techniques for dealing with "difficult" people. They often feel cornered, for example, by a parent or community member, or for that matter by a colleague or a boss who is angry and is relentlessly pressing a demand that seems unreasonable or unrealistic. The result is typically a fight-or-flight response that can spiral into a miserable confrontation that often ends painfully and destructively for everyone. Remembering that when we most need to remain open is when we are least able to do so, let us see how a potentially adversarial interaction can be reframed by the intent of the inquirer to understand interests.

Consider a high school teacher who was approached by a parent concerned about the grade given to his daughter because of a missing paper. The parent begins the conversation by saying, "I want to talk to you about the unfair grade you gave my daughter in your class. It needs to be changed." The first punch has been thrown, and most people in that situation respond defensively when they feel blamed. "There's nothing unfair about it. Your daughter failed to turn in her paper to me. She didn't meet the standards so she got the grade she deserved. I'm not changing it." So it would go with a cycle of blame and defensiveness that would inevitably lead to a complaint being lodged with the principal or district administration.

But a teacher well trained and practiced in inquiry approaches would respond openly, probing for an understanding of the situation from the parent's perspective, with antenna continually searching for the interests that are motivating the parent. This is especially critical before going on record with a position that will trigger an adversarial standoff. Although the teacher is most inclined to close off and become self-protective, he or she opens up the inquiry. The parent has already provided a key interest, that any outcome needs to feel fair. But the teacher continues, even though there is a danger of more personal attacks. "Tell me what you think is unfair about the grade?" This invitation results in a good deal of information. However emotionally and blamefully it is presented, the teacher listens openly and attentively. The following story emerges:

- The student did write the paper. The parent actually read it and had watched the student write it.
- The teacher, rightly or wrongly, has a reputation for being unfair and unreasonable.
- The parent fears that the grade will penalize the student's college ambitions.
- The student placed the paper in the teacher's box in the office. The parent blames the teacher for losing the paper.
- The student would have approached the teacher directly, but felt intimidated.

The teacher's response reflects back the interests that were heard. "So Mr. Jones, you're unhappy with the way you feel your daughter was treated, and you clearly are interested in her success. It also sounds like any solution for you needs to feel fair, should acknowledge the work your daughter actually did, and should not unfairly penalize your daughter for something that you feel might have been my fault." As the teacher watches the parent's response, there will be what Gendlin (1978) calls a *felt sense* that signals that the parent has felt heard. It might take the form of a change in body language, a gesture, facial expression, or remark that communicates in one form or another, "Yes, I think for me it really is about fairness." Based on the parent's reaction, the teacher, as inquirer, will also sense at a gut level that a connection of understanding has been made with the parent. Notice also that the teacher has not agreed with the parent, acknowledged guilt, or promised to change the grade.

Advocating Through Interests

Now the parent is ready, probably for the first time, to genuinely listen to the teacher's perspective. Once again, the teacher communicates through interests, not positions. This will require the teacher to quickly explore his or her own thinking to translate his or her own positions into interests. Table 7.3 illustrates that analysis, which in reality would happen in an instant while the teacher considers a reply. This involves the teacher letting go of rigid perceptions of the situation to understand the core interests that are at work. For example, although the teacher's instinct is to want the situation to go away, the real motivating desire of most teachers is to have a positive and hassle-free relationship with parents. There is a rationale

Table 7.3   Translating Positions Into Interests

Corresponding Interests	*Positions (Mental Models)*
Minimize hassle; Positive relationships with parents	I just wish this parent would go away
Teaching accountability and responsibility	The student did not meet my requirements
Consistency	I do not change grades
Fairness	She got what she deserved

for a tough, hard line approach to this situation, which is to teach accountability and responsibility, and that communicates fairness and consistency. Now the teacher is ready to advocate in a way that communicates the interests and that has the potential to build relationships: "I have some concerns as well that we need to consider. I want to be sure that the way that I grade feels fair and consistent to all my students, and that it is encouraging behavior that teaches students responsibility and accountability for their actions. I wonder if there are some things we could consider doing that might feel fair to all three of us and which could be designed to reward and encourage responsibility."

It would be difficult for a parent to argue with such a reasonable idea, and so the search for the "both/and" would be launched. However, it is important to note that the teacher must also willingly make that transition to a place where such a search is possible. As long as the thinking is closed and fixed, there is little that will break the deadlock, and the conflict will be perpetuated. Once the teacher's interests are understood, it also becomes clear that the "right" stakeholders are not yet in the room. The interest of teaching responsibility (hopefully a shared one) cannot be satisfied until the student joins the problem solving process.

Pointers for Working With Interests

Table 7.4 shows the key elements for working with interests. Remember that these techniques can be very effective, but that they would also need to be constantly practiced for a leader like the teacher in the last example to be able to use them seamlessly and consistently in situations in which fight-or-flight responses are the norm. Teams can support their own training and development by continually thinking together about the interests of all parties that present themselves in a given situation and by pushing back on each other as they strive to understand and separate at a deeper level the differences between positions and interests.

Tools and Techniques

Identifying the Stakeholders

Correct identification of the stakeholders to a problem will increase the likelihood that all interests are taken into account and

Table 7.4   Checklist for Working With Interests

1. Identify the stakeholders and their separate and common interests *(the underlying motivations for what each party wants from the negotiation.)*

2. Clarify the underlying interests by probing the positions (favorite solutions) of all parties.

3. Ask "why?" Interests will often reflect the values of stakeholders, and it is often necessary to probe to uncover the core needs.

4. Look for the separate and common interests for all stakeholders. Discover their interests as well as your own. There are often multiple interests on any topic or issue.

5. Focus on interests (motivations) not positions (favorite solutions).

6. Model learning by inquiring first, and advocating after there has been clear understanding.

7. Interests should be prioritized, to ensure that the most important ones are not lost.

represented during the problem solving process. On the other hand, identifying irrelevant stakeholder groups can lead to real inefficiencies in the process. Broader inclusion is advisable if the issue is complex, will require the cooperation of many groups and individuals in order to be success-

Tools and Techniques

fully addressed, or if the solution must be widely understood. Even if the key stakeholders cannot all be in attendance, it is critical that their interests are identified and considered.

Keep Asking "Why?"

Probe actively in an effort to discover the underlying motivations that people bring to a situation. *The basic rule of thumb:*

- If it sounds like an answer it's probably a position.
- If it sounds like a reason it's probably an interest.

If there is a sense that an identified interest sounds like a solution, ask why it might be a desired outcome. It often takes several levels of asking "why" to understand the true interests.

Tracking the Interests

Make sure that the interests are correctly identified, and never presume to understand another party's interests without checking your assumptions. Make sure that the interests are thoroughly understood by all the stakeholders involved in the issue by discussing each one in turn and giving plenty of time for questions and clarification. Write them clearly for all to see on a chart if you are problem solving in a larger group. Take special note of common interests. It is not unusual in a team problem solving situation like a school faculty or a department staff to have all the interests in common, in which case they will most likely be listed in one column, rather than separated in two or more columns on a T-chart (as, for example, in Figure 7.1). But don't shy away from what appear to be conflicting interests, for their analysis and understanding offer the possibility of deeper appreciation and knowledge of differences. When a T-chart is used, show the common interests with arrows, also as illustrated in Figure 7.1.

Prioritizing Interests

At some point it may be important to prioritize interests. While the relative priority of interests can often be easily identified by group acclamation, when agreement is less apparent, use consensus development techniques to determine priority. It is important that the people who "own" the interests are the ones involved in the prioritization process. Later in the process, when options are evaluated using the interests as the criteria for their appropriateness, it will be helpful to list the interests in prioritized order. Options that fail to meet the top priority interests will be unlikely to form part of the final agreement or solution.

> *See the next two chapters on how to use a prioritized list of interests to help move a group successfully to an agreement.*

SUMMARY

A powerful leader and problem solver should cultivate an ability to inquire deeply into the nature of what motivates people. This discipline requires a willingness to become vulnerable and to understand the world as others see it. It means mindfully letting go of one's own preconceived notions and setting out on a joint search for solutions with others that is focused on possibilities, not limitations. The endeavor is inherently collaborative, and is based on taking responsibility for solving problems and envisioning a future that is inclusive of a set of needs that are much broader than just one's own.

Once those broad needs are thoroughly understood, we are ready to set out with our organizational teams to find a solution that satisfactorily addresses them. That search for solution must continue to keep participants working mutually together on the same page. It should be a naturally creative pursuit, but it can also be a risky one that threatens at any turn to plunge participants back into adversarial fight-or-flight behavior. The next chapter will focus on how to successfully navigate that search in the process of leading through collaboration.

CHAPTER EIGHT

Searching for Solutions

An elementary school staff was unhappy about the conduct of students at lunchtime. They had wrestled with this problem before, and the result had been to tighten the controls on the kids— more rules, more supervision, harsher punishment, and less tolerance of frisky behavior. They got together in a staff meeting to assess the situation, and began for the first time to think deeply about their interests. They realized that they had many interests, as described in the last chapter, but dominating and controlling the students was not on the list. Quite to the contrary, they wanted a system that taught students appropriate behavior, encouraged self-control and responsibility, promoted positive relationships between students and staff, minimized supervision hassles, and supported excellent instruction in the classroom. Their control-oriented solutions had actually undermined many of those interests.

The way the search for solution is conducted is an absolutely critical element of the alchemy that creates true coherence. This very savvy team of educators had tried to throw traditional solutions at a familiar problem, and as a result, little had changed. They had tended to regard the kids as their adversaries on this issue, reacted out of habit, failed to stay focused on what was most important, and neglected their own learning as they worried about the learning of their students. All of these are natural pitfalls for any organization filled with busy people who are preoccupied with other important issues, but who also want to conduct the search for solutions in a way that they will not need to redo it later.

Once that school staff realized that their interests really focused on what they wanted students to learn, they began to think of ways that they could organize lunchtime in order to ensure that they were teaching responsible behavior, promoting positive relationships, minimizing supervision hassles, and supporting excellent instruction. This pointed their creativity in a very different direction. They began to generate options like:

1. Staff takes turns eating lunch with students

2. Play music at lunchtime

3. Increase area for eating to include grass and other areas

4. Students choose eating place (within limits)

5. Playtime prior to eating

6. Students eat in shifts; some play while others eat

7. Assign trash monitors from each room

8. Involve students in managing lunchtime activities

These were a far cry from their habitual response of tightening the rules and supervision, and the solution they finally implemented that combined features from most of the options listed above led to more student responsibility, a more pleasant lunchtime for everyone, and most important, significantly improved behavior in the lunchroom, on the playground, and in the classroom afterwards. There is a real art to ensuring that the search for solutions during collaborative efforts produces an agreement that is consistent with the true organizational vision. That critical and subtle process is the focus of this chapter.

STAYING ON THE SAME PAGE

James Watson, the codiscoverer of DNA, is quoted as saying that "nothing new that is really interesting comes without collaboration" (Schrage, 1995, p. 270). Achieving amazing results is often best accomplished by finding ways of bringing "strange bedfellows" together to create something new. That elementary school staff struggled in part because of the way in which they defined their team. They were a group of adults whose job it was to get the kids to behave, eat a healthy lunch, and be ready to move back into the classroom for an afternoon of productive learning. They had seen themselves as the change agents and the students as their "subjects," and so there was a divide that not only limited the number of problem-solvers, but also limited the way in which the adults approached the problem.

Searching As Allies, Not Adversaries

But they eventually realized they needed to include the whole community in the search for a solution. Once the search shifted from "how can we get those kids to behave during lunchtime?" to "how should we organize lunchtime?" they had lots more help with the problem, and they began to see their quandary very differently. The first question required some level of paternalistic control, whereas the second made room for the possibility that reorganizing the environment might well cause behavioral changes that would be more consistent with the way students were expected to learn at that school.

The search for options should be designed to discover solutions that acceptably address the needs of all key stakeholders, and so the search is framed in a way that keeps everyone searching together collaboratively. Often the most "creative" act in the problem-solving process is finding a way to frame the relationship to see others as allies rather than adversaries.

Eastman Kodak found a way to include archrival Fujifilm in their work with camera manufacturers to establish standards for Advanced Photo System (APS) cameras. The collaboration allowed the companies to save millions that would have been risked with competing standards, and it prevented a situation in which customers would be asked to gamble on competing formats with winners and losers, as in the case of Beta and VHS formats for videocassette recorders.

Many labor relationships have thrived on the realization that partnering is more productive for everyone than the traditional adversarial labor wars. These relationships continue and thrive because the cultures shift to one of partnership, in which each of the key stakeholders—unions, administration and governing body—understands that partnering introduces more productive solutions than fighting or competing.

The same dynamic occurs regularly in school situations in which the parents of special needs students interface with school staff. When they see each other as adversaries, their options are quite positional and the inquiry becomes an either/or. When they successfully cast themselves as partners in advocating for the needs of the student, the walls tend to come down, and the ideas that are generated tend to feel more realistic and acceptable. In an adversarial situation, those same ideas can seem objectionable or even offensive.

MAINTAINING COHERENCE IN THE SEARCH FOR SOLUTIONS

As we have been seeing throughout this book, care must be continually taken to use approaches and techniques that have participants working off the same page, rather than separate pages, remembering

> *Tools and Techniques*

that each of us has a strong tendency to be positional and come into a situation championing our favorite solution on our own separate page. This is true at every stage of the process, including the search for solutions. Figure 8.1 is a checklist for how to lead this process and to ensure that a group's option generation produces a useful list. The rest of the chapter will detail the tools and strategies that maximize the likelihood of success.

Staying Open to Possibilities

As we have been discussing, it is critical that the process of generating possible solutions to organizational problems needs to be

> *See also Chapter 9 for information on the straw design process designed to produce agreements on a single page.*

collaborative and mutual. Remember the physical organization of participants in Figure 3.2 has them arranged so that they can work together off a flipchart, recording each idea at the front of the room. Similarly, there are three key ground rules listed in Figure 8.2 that are particularly helpful in keeping group members working together on a single page. Each will require most participants to reprogram themselves to eliminate habits of human nature that they have probably practiced over a lifetime.

Many readers will recognize the basic rules of brainstorming in Figure 8.2. Each rule serves a vital strategic purpose in keeping the parties working together as a single team, rather than competing

Figure 8.1   Checklist for Generating Options

1. Jointly generate a list of options that are designed to address the identified interests of all the stakeholders *(possibilities the parties can implement together to solve the problem.)*

2. Frame your search to be flexible about how those interests will be met. Strive to find a number of different ways to address the identified needs.

3. Options should be formed and shaped to ensure that each stakeholder's core interests are satisfied, at least acceptably, for example, by targeting each party's risk aversion. What ideas can we find to address each stakeholder's greatest concerns?

4. The framing of the initial problem should have made it easy to identify the difference between current reality and the desired goal as the dynamic tension to be resolved in the problem. Press the group for potential remedies to that tension.

5. Challenge the existing assumptions about what will or will not work, and what might be limiting thinking. Honor risk taking!

6. Option generation should meet the following basic guidelines:
   a. No ownership or attribution—every idea belongs to the whole group.
   b. No evaluation while options are being generated—separate creating from deciding.
   c. No commitment will be assumed or implied on any option until it is explicitly stated.

7. When possible, search for mutually acceptable, objective standards for deciding (independent of the will of the parties) based upon measurability, legitimacy, and impartiality.

8. Push the group to recognize common ground, and anticipate and generate viable, comprehensive, and elegant possibilities for solutions.

"sides." The "no ownership" rule prevents participants from becoming overly attached to options they have generated. A level of detachment preserves objectivity needed in the evaluation and agreements phase to select the best solution to meet the identified needs, rather than anyone's presumed favorite solution. This rule also encourages the generation of options that are responsive to someone else's interests without worrying that something is being offered that cannot be taken back. In fact, in

Tools and Techniques

Figure 8.2   Ground Rules to Frame the Search for Solutions

☐ No ownership—options belong to the group

☐ No evaluation until requested

☐ No commitment will be implied or assumed until stated

polarized situations, many leaders will ask participants to try thinking of options that might be particularly responsive to the *other*
"side's" interests, as a means of encouraging more collaborative
thinking.

Similarly, the "no evaluation" rule pushes against one of our
society's most ingrained habits, which is to judge an idea immediately
after it has been presented. Our penchant for debate and criticism has
us poised to explain the reasons why a given idea will not work, so it
is typical in problem solving for groups to bog down in discussion of
individual ideas as they are generated. This argumentation has at least
two unintended consequences. It distracts participants from the creative process of generating original ideas, and it tends to discourage
new ideas as participants observe the group dumping on their creative
offerings. The Nobel Laureate Linus Pauling once said that the best
way to get a good idea is to come up with a lot of ideas, and so the
process of brainstorming becomes immensely helpful in giving us
access to a bank of possibilities that might acceptably address the
identified needs. I find that the idea that ultimately resolves an issue
often lies somewhere at the bottom of the option list. The goal at this
stage is to encourage a lengthy list of possibilities the group can later
critique and refine, so in the option generation phase we must be
vigilant not to dampen creativity with premature evaluation.

While the "no evaluation" rule keeps participants from rejecting
other people's ideas, the "no commitment" rule helps to keep problem solvers open to additional possibilities. Traditional negotiations
are characterized by an *offer/acceptance* mentality, and negotiators
typically frame their discussion with phrases like the following:

"Here's what I'm willing to do . . ."

"Would you be willing to . . . ?"

"Make me an offer."

Each of these phrases has the effect of locking people into a specific course of action, which closes down the proceedings rather than opening them up. This "no commitment" rule allows everyone to roll up their sleeves and do some "what if we tried" inventing without fear that they are making binding agreements that they might live to regret.

STAYING FOCUSED ON WHAT'S IMPORTANT

We are all "creatures of habit" and justifiably so, given the huge amount of information that bombards us on a daily basis. We base our lives on rituals and patterns to ensure that we are not constantly making trivial decisions related to a wide variety of daily tasks as mundane as remembering to take medications, performing our daily hygiene and cosmetic rituals, or remembering where we parked our cars. While habits serve us well as reminders to floss our teeth each night, they can become a huge obstacle in our search for elegant solutions that require us to break out of habitual ways of seeing the world. Effective problem solvers will exchange those routine behaviors for mindfulness focused on the core interests that are most important to the stakeholders. Remember what happened when the school staff threw habitual control responses at the lunchtime behavior problem that begged for a different kind of approach in order to address the learning needs that lie at the heart of the school's very reason for being.

Breaking the Self-Imposed Rules

Chapters 6 and 7 took an in-depth look at how problem solving must begin with a thoughtful inquiry directed at clarifying the task, as well as to understand what is deeply motivating the stakeholders. If those tasks have been done well, the search for solutions can be carefully and thoughtfully focused on developing ideas that specifically address the underlying problem as well as the most critical needs that have been identified.

A willingness to break traditional patterns—or rules of thinking that bind us to old solutions—and obsolete or unnecessary habits can be crucial to finding better ways to do our business and to solve our thorniest problems. This is the driving force behind the popular concept of "continuous improvement." Our technology industries have proven to be particularly vulnerable to this phenomenon, and so yesterday's darlings, like Apple Computer, America Online, or for that matter Intel or Microsoft, can become tomorrow's "has-beens" unless they are able to continually reinvent themselves.

Our mindless habits form positions or *mental models* that keep us closed off to new possibilities. Ellen Langer, author of *Mindfulness* (1989), challenges us to avoid the trap of unintentional habits that cause us to do things the way we always have. It took the 3M company years to figure out what to do with Post-it notes after they were invented, simply because no one suspected the useful applications in our everyday lives.

Similarly, an elementary school had struggled to get the parents of English language learners actively involved in the school. They tried holding special meetings of that particular parent constituency, many of whom were limited English speakers themselves and unaccustomed to attending school events, and were lucky to attract six people. So they stopped to consider the driving interests around this issue. They realized both staff and parents wanted the same thing: for parents to play an active role in supporting the education of the kids.

They conceived a multicultural storytelling festival with the kids and their families' favorite stories as the main attraction. Kids chose the stories they would perform, sometimes from their family traditions. These were kids who were rarely asked to shine, and they took to the task with a passion and an intensity that surprised everyone. Volunteer tutors spent countless hours helping students to polish those presentations. The first festival attracted 150 parents, most of whom had never been to a school event before. The next year's version brought in well over 200 parents and students, and by that time the whole school was becoming involved with a food and literature festival that celebrated the full diversity of the community. Most important, staff and parent leaders had broken their self-imposed rules about what parent events should be like, to create something bigger, more exciting, and more supportive of student achievement than anyone had thought possible.

Sticking With the Search

Groups also tend to stop working just as soon as one potentially satisfactory solution to a problem has been identified. There may be a number of elegant yet unexplored options, so it is important to continue working long enough to develop many viable possibilities.

If we stop at the first doable idea to come along, we deny ourselves access to even better ones that might have come later. The rules for brainstorming described in Figure 8.2 (no evaluation, ownership or commitment) are designed to help groups stay in an open search for solutions long enough to look in places that they might not otherwise consider, to maximize the chances of finding an elegant and surprising outcome.

Tools and Techniques

Staying Playful

Problem solving, which is often a somber, serious business, also needs to be playful. Laughter, capriciousness, humor, and play (when not allowed to disrupt the process) can be useful tools for breaking through boundaries, which have kept old ways of seeing the world in use. Piggybacking on playful, ambiguous, or "foolish" inspirations can lead to the creation of some very elegant results. George de Mestral is said to have invented Velcro when he set out to fashion a new fastener by "recreating" the natural burdock burrs that stuck to his trousers when he went hunting. Similarly, those school leaders looking for ways of enticing more parents to their meetings got the solution of their dreams when they turned the notion of a meeting upside down. Once a sufficiently exciting array of possibilities has been generated to address the identified needs, then closure strategies can be used to clarify, organize, evaluate, and refine the list as problem solvers move to an acceptable solution.

Tools and Techniques

When Too Many Is Not Such a Good Thing

While I have touted the usefulness of brainstorming in developing a list of possible solutions to a problem, the process has some practical limitations related to efficiency and effectiveness. Too often it seems that groups are surprised and disappointed that their efforts to solve a thorny problem have failed, especially because of the time and effort they have spent generating a lengthy list of possible solutions, whether or not they are relevant to the identified needs.

See Chapter 9 for more about reaching closure.

All too often we allow the search for solution to digress into a search for *any* solution, versus one that will meet each of our critical needs acceptably. We become powerful and successful problem solvers when we understand *everyone's* interests at a deep level and when the search for inventive approaches is directed to address all the needs acceptably. For this reason the brainstorming options do not encourage quantity over quality. As Robert Fritz (1991) suggests, we are most effective at creating something new when the options we generate are very carefully targeted to meet the identified needs.

Approaches to Option Generation, or Brainstorming

Tools and Techniques

There are a variety of ways to generate and capture options. The following approaches offer distinctively different tools for eliciting ideas from a group:

The Freewheeling Method

In this more traditional approach to brainstorming, everyone calls out their ideas as they think of them. The ideas are written down on flipcharts. This method is quick, but less inclusive and less likely to produce thorough results.

Nominal Group Technique (NGT)

In this approach designed to cultivate broader involvement, participants spend a few moments thinking and writing silently, and then take turns offering their ideas—or passing if they don't have an idea when their turn comes. This method ensures that group members who are more reserved have an equal opportunity to contribute. The process continues, in rounds, until everyone passes. The same method can be used to combine small group work into a larger group setting. Ask small groups to report one idea at a time, continuing around the room for as many rounds as necessary until the ideas or the available time is exhausted. This method works well anytime there is an interest in eliciting ideas from individuals (for example, asking members of a group to share ideas for behaviors that are impeding group effectiveness).

Affinity Charting

This approach helps the group to sort a complex array of ideas even as they are generated. Participants write their ideas down on cards, or "Post-it" notes, and the facilitator assists them in collecting the contributions on the flipchart or a wall in appropriate subject-clusters. This method works well for quickly categorizing, or recategorizing, large amounts of data. Use it for analyzing very complex issues with many different viewpoints to be captured, or if people do not want to make their own personal views public.

IN GENERATING OPTIONS, ADDRESS THE POINTS OF GREATEST FRICTION

There are also some important techniques that go with option generation that serve to keep the parties from polarizing, or to bring them back from an impasse. For examples, often when there is a tough issue on the table or when a group finds itself stuck and headed to an impasse there is fear involved for more than one stakeholder that relates to losing something important, whether resources, control, values, or the perception of fairness. That *risk aversion* can be sensitive, and there may be reluctance by all parties to address it. But addressing people's greatest sense of vulnerability also provides a direct line to the interests and options that will be a driving force in resolving the situation. So the search for solutions should explore inventive ways of lessening the perceived risks.

Identify the Perceived Risks

This risk aversion can be identified and addressed in several useful ways. A thoughtful and rational analysis of the fears that have a stakeholder refusing to accept an agreement will usually provide the clues that are needed to alleviate those concerns. Understanding where and why we are self-protective enables us to generate options that allow us to be less defensive and more open. Assume in this context that your partners in any kind of negotiation cannot say yes until their risk aversion has been identified and resolved. For example, the parent of a

Tools and Techniques

special needs student may be resisting a program recommendation that involves a change in teachers because the student is happy with the current teacher, and the parents are fearful that the student may not like the new teacher as much. The program modification could include a commitment to pilot the program for two weeks, or to arrange a special opportunity for the student to spend time with the unfamiliar teacher before moving into the new classroom.

Safeguard the Interests

Any actual agreement that is reached also needs to assure each of the parties that their interests will be substantially secured by the outcome. Entering into an agreement on a wish and a prayer is foolish if the fears you bring to a problem are significant. A fire chief was concerned about an idea that would allow firefighters serving as paramedics to arrange shift trades with nonparamedics. But every shift must include minimum staffing of paramedics, so unlimited trade rights might expose the department to overtime costs that couldn't be controlled. An acceptable solution to this problem had to include some sort of agreement that addressed management's perceived risk related to financial exposure. The union leaders in that instance became powerful problem solvers by understanding the risk aversion that was involved on both sides, and by helping managers to generate options that address those rubs. Managers would have been negligent in agreeing to anything that did not adequately ensure that they would be fiscally responsible, so rather than stonewalling the issue, they focused their energy in a search for approaches that addressed both sets of needs. Ultimately the pilot program they set up worked well, and it has continued without increasing costs.

Tools and Techniques

When people become self-protective, options must be generated that allow them to make commitments that they are certain will be kept. This means not only thinking about *how to solve the problem*, but also determining *how to ensure* that the solution will actually resolve the identified concerns. A failure to figure out how to secure the commitments will often doom the entire effort. In our example in Chapter 7, management and the union were stuck on the issue of who would be on standby for call back on after-hours emergencies. Management wanted mandatory standby for everyone, and the union wanted it to be voluntary. The informal risk analysis revealed that management was fearful that there would not be adequate coverage, and the union worried that employees who lived farther away would be forced to return for mundane emergencies that involved hours of driving for a 15 minute repair. The solution addressed both sets of fears. Employees voluntarily formed and managed a standby pool to ensure that there was adequate coverage for after-hours emergencies. They also agreed that if at some point there was no longer adequate coverage on a voluntary basis, then management could impose a mandatory system. Each party's fear, or risk aversion, was adequately addressed by the outcome.

SEARCH FOR EXTERNAL STANDARDS OF FAIRNESS

Many years ago I sold a used car to a close friend. Our conversation hemmed and hawed, back and forth with no concrete ideas being generated by either of us for fear that we would say or do something that would offend the other. Neither of us wanted the price of the car to end up imposing itself negatively on our relationship. Each of us wanted to establish

Tools and Techniques

a fair price for the car, if only to ensure that the other one felt fine about it. So we turned to the "Kelley Blue Book," which gave us relatively neutral information on valuing a car. I have long forgotten what the price was, but we somehow managed to agree on an amount that got the deal done and kept the friendship intact.

People will often be reluctant to say yes to an option without some assurance that it will be a fair one. This is particularly true in situations in which money is an issue. The search for solutions should include a hunt for mechanisms that will assure everyone that what is being considered is fair and legitimate, which should foster the sense of partnership discussed earlier. This search will be a creative and divergent inquiry, and the results will need to be analyzed just like any other list of options to determine which of the potential criteria, if any, acceptably address the identified interests. For example, the following list of options represents standards that might be applied to determine the fair price of a used computer:

1. The price of comparable computers selling in the newspaper classified ads

2. How much does the same computer sell for on eBay?

3. Ask a computer shop to appraise the computer

4. Check Web sites that list the value of comparable computers, and average the prices listed

5. Depreciate the initial price of the computer and accessories by 20% per year to correspond to an expected life span of five years based on the longest period either of us has kept a computer in the past

The same principle applies to negotiating compensation in a labor agreement. When labor and management can find a way to get money "off the table" it frees them up for conversations about more important things, like how to improve the quality of work that is done in the organization. I have seen many different standards used to determine a fair way to allocate compensation:

- Comparability with similar organizations or similar jobs
- Linking compensation to year-end balances and reserves
- Maintaining the same percentage of salaries in respect to total revenues over time
- Linking increases in compensation to increases in organizational revenues
- Relating compensation changes to the federal consumer price index (CPI)

No criteria will work in every situation, but finding standards that will work in a given circumstance can do wonders for defusing a volatile situation. Nineteen years ago I was part of a group of school district labor and management negotiators who developed a formula for salary compensation that was based on maintaining the same percentage of certain income sources over time. While it may not be prudent for it to last forever, that mechanism for "getting money off the table" is still in effect as of this writing, though the individuals who participated in the initial agreement have changed a number of times and the formula itself has also changed. Adopting a formula has freed up the labor and management energy to focus on far more important issues—like improving instruction—with more confidence that compensation has been fairly resolved.

FOCUS RELENTLESSLY AND
COURAGEOUSLY ON THE QUEST

A key predictor of success in creating coherence is the "perspiration factor" based on the commitment of the participants themselves. A determined commitment to thoughtfully understand a problem and the various interests—and to search relentlessly for a solution—delivers powerful and effective results. It is not always pretty or easy, but the more people who have that focus and passion the better the chances of producing successful, coherent results. Michael Shrage connects the coherence and perspiration principles as he extols the virtue of the collaborative search for solution, however messy it gets:

> There's an alchemical, almost mystical quality to the best of these collaborations; a sense of creation that transcends individual talent and skill. You can hear it in a Rodgers and Hart musical or a Lennon and McCartney song. Yet there's nothing inherently fragile about the process: some of the most productive collaborations occur at the top of the participants' lungs. . . . To be successful, a collaboration can't afford the risk of substituting euphemisms for clarity. Collaborative relationships aren't built on rudeness; it's just that they won't let good manners get in the way of a good argument. (Schrage, 1995, pp. 34–35)

Once the interests are in clear focus, and the main points of resistance have been identified, the solutions are reached through dogged, stubborn determination. This is the stuff on which much of the organizational leadership and change literature is based. Much has been written about Thomas Edison's tireless search through hundreds of possible materials for a light bulb filament before he found one that worked. Similarly, the "continuous improvement" and "total quality" movements are based on tireless pursuit of a better way to do things.

Seek Ways of "Expanding the Pie"

This also means looking past perceived limitations to find ways of "expanding the pie." This often involves having a deep enough understanding of all the needs and resources in the system so that solutions can be found in surprising places. Years ago, my school district was renting out surplus property to a health club that at the time was asking for some lease concessions. Because there were no other prospective tenants in sight, the board was reconciled to accepting the club's conditions. However, we knew that the unions had long asked for a health and wellness benefit, so it was suggested that the district approach the club about ways that discounts could be provided to school employees. The club readily agreed to some attractive discounts, because it provided them a large pool of possible new members, and other clubs in town soon followed suit to stay competitive. A frustrating situation became a more favorable one for the district and the health club as we found other ways of extracting value from the relationship.

Earlier in this chapter, I told the story of the elementary school that had struggled to get traditionally uninvolved parents to participate in school events. What started with only a few parents attending a meeting became a transformational approach to create the oral history and cultural festival that eventually yielded hundreds of participants they never used to see. Rather than giving up and assuming that it cannot be done, the principal and staff held firm to their vision for parental engagement and, through a focused intent to create something new, found an elegant way to meet their interests that really surprised everyone.

Honoring Risk Taking (Creative Courage)

I have worked for many years with a city that had really stressed the importance of staff utilizing problem-solving approaches to address issues with each other, with contractors and developers, and with the community. We generally found the top leaders in the city supportive of these approaches and practicing them in thorny situations, even to the extent of calling for help when they felt that a problem was too complex to tackle alone. But fascinatingly, whenever we met with employees in workshops designed to create that capacity for problem solving, they would express fear, doubts, and suspicions about whether or not proactive decision making is truly honored in the organization. They would frequently point to examples in which they perceived some form of punishment or retribution to employees who made mistakes or who tried to stretch for a solution that, for one reason or another, may have seemed in conflict with the boss's favored way of doing business.

Ours is a culture that celebrates success. Unfortunately, that is often interpreted as intolerance of failure or of dissent. A department with a 100% success rate at implementing new innovations is probably not learning as much as another department with a 50% success rate, if the former are innovating 90% less. The search for creative solutions is about learning, which entails the establishment of a culture that values a cycle of innovation and reflection. That will encourage or even demand yet another round of creating. To that end, the organization must cultivate what Rollo May (1975) calls "creative courage."

> Whereas moral courage is the righting of wrongs, creative courage, in contrast, is the discovering of new forms, new symbols, new patterns on which a new society can be built . . . the creative artist and poet and saint must fight the *actual* (as contrasted to the ideal) gods of our society—the god of conformism as well as the gods of apathy, material success, and exploitative power. These are the "idols" of our society that are worshipped by multitudes of people. (pp. 13–23)

Many colleagues, in fact, ironically reinforce conformity, at the same time that they demand excellence. Groups with clearly established ideas typically exemplify May's social "idols" in workplace relations and habits related to the way things should be. This specifically inhibits creativity and group learning if, for example, a new member of a faculty team learns from the veterans on the faculty or from the boss that either a certain outcome is expected or "we don't do things that way around here."

In an inquiry approach emphasizing creativity, many of the elegant solutions have not yet been invented. Parameters need to be broad enough—and focused specifically on interests—to ensure that the problem solvers or negotiators have the latitude to be creative in the search for solutions. The creators, in turn, need to keep their constituencies well informed so there is ample time for all stakeholders to become comfortable with the innovations and to help verify that their interests are being well met.

Separate Creating and Deciding

In this regard, it is critical to separate the processes of creating and deciding. It is very important to establish norms that honor creativity and risk taking during the search for solutions to critical problems. If those new faculty members get the message from the veterans that their ideas are not valued or honored, then their creativity will be stunted or eliminated. Recently a national governmental official was asked to resign because of an idea that he had suggested. Whatever one's opinion might be of the idea itself, such a response runs the risk of solving a problem by creating an even bigger one.

Tools and Techniques

Firing or disciplining the person who generates an idea sends a potentially chilling message throughout the organization, "don't be too creative around here, because if someone important doesn't like your idea, you might be fired." This organizational reaction seems almost guaranteed to stifle creative thinking and deny the organization access to the creative processes that it most needs to move forward effectively. The real accountability might be better directed to the decision makers that move to closure on an idea without ample constituent support, than to the person who originally generated the idea.

Leaders must take care that the process of deciding is distinctly separated from the process of creating. The "no commitment" and "no evaluation" rules are designed to give problem solvers a chance to think creatively without the evaluative constraints that might impede inventive thinking. Discourage problem solvers from leaping too quickly to agreement or even offers until they have had ample opportunity to explore the possibilities. The interests that inspired the search will also prove their value later when it comes time to narrow down the choices and decide on a course of action. Trust that the process will eventually protect decision makers from making bad choices, and discourage them from evaluating until the deciding phase begins.

SUMMARY

The search for solutions is one of the most enjoyable aspects of leadership, as a group sets out divergently to find an elegant way of satisfying the identified needs. The leader's mission at this point is to keep participants working together as one team that is open to creative possibilities, to keep them focused on the areas of greatest need and the points of greatest friction, and to keep the process inventive and playful. This is the place where the real benefits of collaboration and consensus come into play. By interacting with each other and thinking about old ideas in inventive new ways, something original can be created that has the potential of addressing all the needs acceptably. With access to a rich and creative list of possibilities, the team can begin the convergent part of the process and move carefully and comfortably to a resolution. That stage of narrowing things down and moving to agreement is the focus of Chapter 9.

CHAPTER NINE

Reaching Effective Agreements

SECURING THE TRUST

There will undoubtedly be readers eager to "get to the bottom line" who might even skip to this chapter and read it first. If you are one of those individuals, my purpose here is to advise you that many of the fundamentals needed to guide a group to closure have already been presented in the preceding pages. While there are some very efficient process tools designed to help structure group work more effectively and even to mediate groups who inadvertently find themselves at an impasse near decision time, the best way to bring a collection of individuals to an agreement is to start it off right in the first place—attending thoughtfully to the community, keeping stakeholders and their constituents on one page, focusing on what is most important, and searching creatively for approaches that will satisfy all the core interests acceptably. If these things have been done well, then the "magic" of coherence will be at work, and an agreement ought to be close at hand.

Closure begins when the group is first convened, and the best way to ensure that decisions will be made effectively is to bring people together in a way that allows them to share each other's interests and to trust each other to make decisions that will respect those needs and to fix it if a decision does not accomplish what was expected or promised. When a group comes to see themselves as allies focused together on a common goal, they can begin to relax about decisions because they know that there will be ample opportunity to improve them as they go. When mistrust of motives and interpersonal competitiveness prevails, the act of deciding becomes like the final two minutes of a championship game—competitive and nerve-wracking as each participant jockeys for position. Though the approaches listed below are helpful in addressing impasse, they are more powerful if initiated before polarization occurs.

LISTENING FOR THE COMMON GROUND

My partner and I were asked to facilitate a community meeting that was intended to reach agreement on the best response to a problem related to day laborers who were soliciting work from contractors along several city blocks. Participants in the meeting numbered about 40 and included community development staff, law enforcement personnel, educators, neighbors, interested community members, business representatives, social service people, day laborers, and interpreters, among others. The task had a number of issues that needed to be addressed, including safety, law enforcement, education, traffic, social services, how work is allocated, and the neighborhood environment, to name a few. These issues were controversial and divisive, and included passionate perspectives related to the quality of life in the neighborhood and the kinds of services offered to undocumented workers.

We set aside the better part of the day for our session, and the process of telling the story and understanding interests took several hours. By the time we had finished generating options, we had a list with over seventy possibilities and just a little over an hour left in the meeting. But my partner and I, as well as many of the other participants, also realized at this point that the conversations we had heard over the course of the day were richly laced with evidence of common ground in the thinking among the stakeholders. That is, a high level of coherence had been created, and simply needed to be named and summarized. We took a 20-minute break in the formal meeting and invited anyone who wanted to help to join us at the flipcharts to develop a straw design that would detail a plan for how to move forward. The result of that spontaneous committee's work was a 10-point approach to the problem that set forth the steps to be taken to address the issues we had identified. The group modified the work somewhat and left the room on schedule with a consensus plan that was approved by the city council and was ultimately implemented in the community.

Whereas this particular story illustrates a situation in which we were able to bypass some of the conventional tools and techniques for moving groups through the process of agreement, it also demonstrates what can be accomplished simply through careful and constructive listening. You may recall the discussion in Chapter 1 about learning to listen to groups differently, as we might learn to listen to jazz or classical music in a way that sharpens our ability to understand. An ear that has been finely tuned to notice and track the common ground is in my experience the single most useful skill in producing coherent agreements in groups. In some ways this runs counter to our culture, which seems wired to focus on and argue about differences, rather than to identify and build agreements around similarities.

A powerful, consensus oriented leader will develop an ear for how different perspectives fit together, focusing on areas of agreement versus separateness. Even pro-choice or right-to-life advocates have many areas in which they agree; for example, preventing unwanted pregnancies. Understanding how perspectives overlap can help us notice the possibilities for solution, which is far more productive than obsessing on the likelihood of impasse. I have noticed that this is especially helpful (e.g., in school situations in dealing with the demands of angry or disgruntled parents). Thoughtful inquiry into the nature of the complaint will often reveal core interests that hold the promise of a solution. A demand for a specific remedy—such as changing a grade or reversing the decision of a teacher or administrator—is often a plea for meaningful mechanisms for involving the parent in educational decisions. For example, one parent (who was probably seen by the school as problematic) was able to understand how his passionate advocacy often crossed the line into harassment. He was satisfied with agreements that stipulated who the parent could see with a problem, and how he would back off if given feedback by school officials that he was crossing the line. Crucial to the agreement is the ability of school staff to listen to the complaints and hear core, common ground interests in a strong working relationship that supports the success of the student.

MAKING THINKING VISIBLE AND NAMING DILEMMAS

Problem solving on really thorny issues is often a rocky journey, involving a trip through what has been called "the valley of despair" before a group emerges to the promised land that is an elegant and compliance-prone agreement. There is a lot that a leader can do to shepherd problem solvers along on the journey when they get bogged down in conflict or impasse. Much has already been said throughout this book about the value of openness in creating coherence in a team. That quality can be instrumental in delivering group decisions that work.

Let me give an example of how openly addressing the problem can pull polarized parties back on to the same team and propel them forward toward a viable agreement. In Chapter 3, I discussed the notion of an "undiscussable" issue as a taboo topic that the group tiptoes around for fear that it might get messy. Generally, when a group is polarized or at an impasse, things are already messy. Avoiding the polarization out of fear that the adversarial positions will resurface only compounds the mistrust and the unpleasantness. We found just such polarization between a school district and a charter school that featured a dual-immersion Spanish-English language program in which students received the vast majority of their instruction in Spanish for the first several grades. School staff members were passionately committed to the dual-immersion program out of a deep belief in the research that offered compelling academic, social, cultural, and career benefits to students who could become bilingual, if only they were given enough time. District staff members were committed to the broad benefits of a program that produced bilingual students, as well as to doing whatever needed to be done to ensure that all students, particularly English learners, perform acceptably under the mandates of the high-stakes accountability systems imposed by the state and federal governments. There were questions about how much more time could be invested in a system that did not promise to deliver successful academic results for all students on the mandated English language assessments that did not afford the luxury of time.

There was animosity between the parties, with steadily worsening relationships, until they laid out their thinking and named the dilemma that was dividing them. They finally acknowledged to each other that they had allowed themselves to assume that a desire to maintain the purity of dual immersion was incompatible with the goal of ensuring that English learners perform well on high-stakes tests by the second grade. Why not work together to find a way to have both? Once they satisfied themselves that everyone, in fact, wanted both, it became possible to sit down together and agree on modifications to the language mix as well as to the way that instruction was delivered, to at least maximize the *possibility* for both to occur. This is an example of the reframing by leaders that must take place in the third quadrant of Figure 3.4 for groups to move to generative engagement and to produce powerful collaborative results.

Getting Unstuck

A group is often naturally inclined to polarize around positions. A skillful leader can help group members move away from a focus on the differences, or *either/or* perspectives, toward integration based on legitimate common ground reflected by a *both/and* point of view. A conscious effort to open up thinking and name the dilemmas a group is wrestling

Tools and Techniques

with enables members to create shared meaning about their common condition and to ensure that their conversations support their ability to work together through difficult issues toward mutually acceptable outcomes.

As mentioned in Chapter 6, identifying a problem clearly and rationally makes it possible for the parties to a dispute to frame it as a common goal rather than a deep division. Naming the dilemma in a way that "draws the circle around the entire team" can make an intimidating conflict seem less emotional and more accessible for analysis and problem solving by integrating the group's thinking instead of continuing divisiveness or adversarialism. In this way, the most powerful problem solvers from both the district and charter school could actively engage with each other in the search for elegant options to meet everyone's needs, not just their own. It required the leaders to clearly and distinctly reiterate that they needed "to work together to find a way to ensure that we effectively meet the needs of our English learners without sacrificing the immense benefits of the dual-immersion program." Everyone must be able to trust that the leaders will not compromise on the need to discover and generate possibilities that will address *all* of the perspectives. A strong commitment to emerge with outcomes that resolve the conflict effectively and that build the relationship allows participants to give up their own position in favor of participation in that joint search. Accordingly, a leader who is both consensus and solution oriented must have the ability and the courage to push the group through impasse.

UNDERSTANDING CONSENSUS

The coherence principle is based on the dynamic that is involved in aligning a group by allowing its members to communicate and problem solve in a way that creates shared meaning around the subject at hand. In its ideal form, this results in consensus among group members, but it is possible to achieve an acceptable level of coherence without actually achieving consensus. This means that a leader who is charged with bringing a group to an agreement needs to have a sophisticated understanding of the dynamics of consensus and how they might impact the quest for agreement. In this context, there are three critical guidelines to consensus that are indicated in Table 9.1 and discussed later.

Tools and Techniques

Table 9.1   Consensus Guidelines

---

1. Know what it is

2. Decide in advance what you will do if you cannot reach it

3. Know when to use it

Know What Consensus Is

Usually when members of the same work group are asked if they know what consensus is, many of them will answer affirmatively. But when pressed for their definitions, they often give conflicting answers, such as:

- Everyone agrees
- Most people agree
- A majority agrees
- 80% agree
- Nobody disagrees violently

It does not matter so much what the definition is, so long as the group agrees on a definition in advance, for obvious reasons. If a group is aspiring for consensus, and some think that everyone must agree, and others think that only half the group plus one must agree, the group is setting itself up for some pretty serious conflict down the road.

Table 9.2 sets forth a definition of consensus that is consistent with a problem solving approach that aspires to create coherence.

Table 9.2   Consensus

Everyone in the group can support and live with the decision.
In the end, everyone can say: "I believe you understand my point of view and my interests, and I believe I understand yours. Whether or not I prefer this decision above all others, I will support it because my core interests were acceptably addressed, and it was reached fairly and openly."

Adapted from William Ouchi (1981, p. 43).

Clearly, this definition depends on a principled discussion that feels fair and open and that produces authentic understanding of the interests that are driving any given decision. Sometimes everyone will be equally committed to one particular idea, and sometimes there will be participants who are less enthusiastic than others, but who can go along with the decision. A sound consensus may have been reached if 75% of the group actively supports the decision and the rest can accept it. Only in rare instances involving impasse around a highly charged issue when all other plausible solutions have been explored is it advisable to accept a decision that has less than half the participants actively embracing an outcome. One elementary school faculty left a meeting thinking they were at an impasse, only to find that they had an agreement when this definition was proposed the next day. It gave the dissenters the comfort they needed to know that their interests would be honored in the pilot implementation.

Consensus Definitions From the Quaker Tradition

This concept of consensus also demands that participants in the process have a strong commitment to the integrity of the group. Often, broad ownership is as important as the actual decision. A teacher whose school district had been a client of mine for a number of years shared with me two additional definitions from the Quaker tradition that help to refine an understanding of what consensus is, and why it is used. "Consensus is a process used to find the highest level of agreement *without* dividing the participants into factions," and "Consensus decision making requires us to be tough minded and tenacious—to the process, the vision, the interests, and the community, not to our positions or ideas." These definitions, when clarified in advance with a group, can be especially useful in keeping the space in a way that keeps all participants committed to their collective goals, and working in a collaborative fashion to seek an elegant agreement that will meet everyone's needs acceptably.

Decide in Advance What You Will Do If You Cannot Reach Consensus

Even in those situations in which decision makers decide to attempt consensus, there needs to be some thought given to what will happen if a group cannot reach it. In *Democracy in America,* the 1835 masterpiece by Frenchman Alexis de Tocqueville, he warned of a phenomenon that he termed "tyranny of the majority" in which the minority in a democracy is dominated by the wishes of the majority (de Tocqueville, 2000, pp. 238–249). A group aspiring to consensus can suffer an even more difficult phenomenon in which a few dissidents can frustrate the wishes of the majority by refusing to agree to a consensus viewpoint. We have observed this occurrence in a number of school situations in which the desire of most faculty members to implement a certain innovation like a new bell schedule or a new parent conferencing format is frustrated by a dissenter who is unhappy about the proposed change.

The antidote is simple, but for the sake of fairness must be implemented in advance of the problem solving process. The group should agree on a time limit, like the end of the meeting or a certain date, and it should determine a fallback method that will be implemented in the event that a consensus decision has not been reached. That might involve any of the following:

Tools and Techniques

- Majority vote
- Status quo

- Manager decides
- Third party decides
- Committee decides
- Luck decides (toss a coin)

A dissenter will work much harder to ensure that her interests are addressed by a potential solution if she knows that there may be a vote and she is likely to wind up on the losing end. This rule allows for a vigorous discussion and it enables participants to move on when a decision point is reached. Groups with a high trust relationship can engage in vigorous discussions that are rich with dissenting perspectives and ensure a thorough exploration of the issues, and they can still trust one another to make a decision that is best for the organization. In this spirit, our own seven-member school board, that makes most of their decisions by consensus, has agreed that split votes are a healthy expression of the democratic process, and the board members support the outcomes, regardless of whether it reflects a consensus agreement.

Know When to Use Consensus

By its very nature, consensus is a time-consuming process, so unilateral command and control decision making is generally the best approach when lives are at stake in an emergency situation, such as a fire rescue response, as discussed in Chapter 6. However, it seems nothing is ever simple in decision making. I have learned from experienced firefighters that an optimal approach in an urgent situation often varies significantly from pure, autocratic decision making. When a crew responds to an emergency scene, it is impossible to know exactly what circumstances await them when they arrive. Depending on what they find, it may be that the most junior member of the crew, for example the paramedic, may have the most knowledge and expertise on the particular emergency that they are facing. An officer may take a few extra moments to triage the scene through a mini-consultation before issuing orders to mobilize the crew. Or the more senior crewmembers may defer to the paramedic if the situation demands immediate medical attention.

Any decision making approach needs to match the situation, and a critical skill is recognizing when to use a given method. While there

Table 9.3   Key Decision-Making Variables

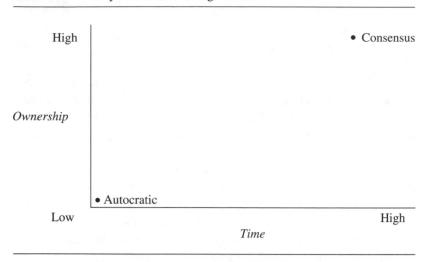

are a number of considerations, two important workplace factors involve the amount of *time* it takes and the degree of *ownership* or constituent involvement that is desired in the decision. Table 9.3 depicts a graph that plots those variables for consensus and autocratic approaches. We traditionally plot consensus in the upper right-hand corner of the chart (high/high), and autocratic/unilateral in the lower left (low/low). Everyone's ideal place to be, of course, would be in the upper left quadrant (low time, high ownership), the elusive holy grail of decision making. However, there are strategies that can move both consensus and unilateral decision making into that upper-left quadrant. For example, agreeing to utilize luck as a decision making model can be quite effective, especially in low-level decisions. Who kicks off first in the Super Bowl is quickly and easily resolved because the parties agree in advance to tossing a coin and letting the winner choose. It is fast, and there is a high level of support for the decision. This obviously only works on less important decisions.

Few people would be willing, for example, to turn over issues in a collective bargaining negotiation to chance. However, they often agree to third party arbitration as a means of settling thorny disputes. I was once involved in a potentially divisive grievance over a teacher transfer issue that we quickly resolved by taking the paperwork of the four internal candidates to the high school in a neighboring district and asking the principal, department chair, and a teacher to look over the applications and tell us which teacher was best qualified. If the grievant was selected, we agreed that he would get the next available opening. If any of the other candidates were selected, it was agreed that the grievance would be dropped, and that is in fact what happened. The decision was made relatively quickly and had a very high level of ownership, including the grievant who felt he got a fair hearing!

PLANNING FOR DECISION MAKING

Spending quality time in advance discussing the optimal approach to decision making can shorten the amount of time required and increase the ownership. Those teams of firefighters I described above increase their ownership in unilateral decision making by spending time in advance clarifying together roles and expectations in the decision making process. Clear communications and a trusting relationship can empower decision makers in some circumstances to decide effectively on behalf of the group.

Organizing Decision Making and Communications to Save Time

A group willing to invest some time thinking about what kinds of decision making to use in a given situation, and who should participate, can save a lot of decision time down the line. An effective communications system can make this even easier. It is possible to devote valuable meeting time to dialogue on the most critical issues if there are mechanisms in place that are faithfully accessed for staying in touch with

Tools and Techniques

the group on routine items. This can be an e-mail, voice mail, bulletin, or newsletter in which members communicate information, agenda items, and routine announcements. This also makes it possible for people to empower others to act on their behalf if they know that issues of some controversy will be posted first and that they can reserve the right to participate in a decision that they care about somewhere down the line. This also presumes a group expectation that if people empower others to act, they will support the decision that is reached, and, in the reflection process, help them to learn and improve the outcome in the future.

In my own school district, we were eager to involve principals in more of the management decisions made in the district level administrative team, but we were also concerned about the time commitments involved. For some time, principals rotated into those meetings, but it was a matter of chance that principals who happened to be in attendance at a given meeting had an interest in the items under discussion. So we implemented a new system in which we publish the agendas in advance via e-mail, and anyone with an interest in a given item self-invites to the meeting. This way we have the people in the room that care about the item, and principals only need to attend the meetings that are important to them. Many meetings have additional participants who self-select items from the published agenda, which we adjust to get those items done first so they can return to their work sites as soon as possible. Most importantly, there is more knowledge and ownership of our decisions because everyone generally has the opportunity to be aware of what is being considered, and to participate if desired.

The Group Decision Making Profile

Planning for decision making should include giving some thought, not only to who participates, but also to how decisions will be made. We have found that most work groups that take the trouble to have such a conversation prefer to delegate more routine operational decisions to the group leader, or a leadership team, and reserve consensus decision making for the most strategically important issues. A decision making profile will take into account, for example, the amount of time available and the level of ownership that is needed in any given decision. If communication systems are such that people can invite themselves into decisions they are strongly interested in, even greater efficiencies are realized. Table 9.4 shows some common decision making approaches and situations in which they are most useful. Many groups find it helpful to think in advance about these different approaches to decision making, and when each might be most useful.

Thus a group can plan in advance how decision making is framed by asking itself some of the following questions:

- Is the decision/issue important enough to justify the investment of everyone's time?
- Do we need broad ownership?
- Is it related to our core reason for being (vision and interests)?
- Can/should someone else be empowered to act?
- Can those with an interest be given access to the decision making without necessarily involving everyone?

Table 9.4   Planning Decision Making

Some Common Approaches	When to Use Each Approach
Consensus	On strategically important issues when there is ample time to reach agreement.
Autocratic (unilateral or top-down)	Important, time-sensitive matters such as a safety issue, or less important operational issues that have been delegated to a single decision-maker or a committee.
Autocratic plus consultation	The same as autocratic, when more ownership is desired and there is insufficient time to produce a consensus.
Majority voting	Important issues in which there is insufficient time to reach consensus, and when the ownership of most participants is desirable, as in the case of a democratic election. This is also a useful "fallback" to consensus.
Third party	When there is an important issue that is likely to get stuck at impasse, and when some commonly held standard of fairness is desirable, as in the case of a judge, jury, or arbitrator.
Luck/chance	On less important issues when fairness is more important than ownership of the decision, as in drawing straws or tossing a coin.

Advanced thought on the purpose of the decision can save large amounts of time as participants think about the most appropriate way to address the situation.

REDUCING THE LIST OF OPTIONS

With a commitment to move toward consensus and the development of a great list of options as described in Chapter 8, the problem solving team can initiate the convergent part of the process. This involves conversation and a set of process structuring tools that will help to organize a group's work around consensus. This is the phase of the problem solving process that provides an opportunity to evaluate the potential for a given option or set of options to elegantly address the needs of every stakeholder.

Winnowing the List of Options

When there is a rich, raw list of options, the group wants to begin reducing the list to those options that will be the most viable. This winnowing can be done after there has been a thorough discussion of options and interests, or the list reduction and analysis can be done simultaneously.

The first cut of the list, also sometimes known as the "call for the thumbs," provides a general sense of the group's views on any individual item. The facilitator leads the group through the list, asking members to give a thumb up, thumb down, or thumb neutral sign. The group can also eliminate duplication and combine similar ideas at this point. The rules for this winnowing process are listed in Table 9.5.

Tools and Techniques

Table 9.5   Instructions for the Winnowing Process

1. Rather than voting on whether they personally like a given item, group members should be asked to envision whether the option is likely to be part of the solution according to the interests expressed. This helps prevent positionalism and keeps participants thinking more globally.

2. A general number of "thumbs down" will result in the facilitator removing that item from the list (except in the event of rule #3 below). The actual number is arbitrary, but can be generally defined as "all but a few."

3. Even if an item is "voted" down, if any one member of the group feels strongly that the item should remain on the list for further discussion, it will remain on the list.

4. Items which collect unanimous thumbs up should be specially marked, or placed on an "honor roll" list of items that can make up the foundation of a straw design. Remind the group that this does not mean that the item has been "voted in," but rather that all participants envision that item might plausibly be part of the solution set.

While it is hoped that this process might result in a significant reduction in the number of items, it is not unusual for groups to leave most ideas on the list at this stage. The process will be successful if the group achieves a better understanding of each option, and a sense of which are the most intriguing.

Recording Tip

As the group moves through the list of options, mark them by crossing out discardable options, and starring the unanimous items or placing them on a special list. If the group has used the winnowing tools, most of the starred items (the "honor roll") will be included in early straw designs.

Weighted Polling

This technique provides a quantified way of assessing the group's preferences by developing a "scattergram" indicating how the top priority items are arranged. This technique is *not* intended to produce a final vote on the issue, but to give information about the most popular ideas. While there are many possible variations to this method, the basic steps are listed in Table 9.6.

Tools and Techniques

Sample Weighted Polling

During labor negotiations, a city and a firefighters union decided to identify a new group of cities to use for comparison of salary and benefits. After a list of possible characteristics for selecting comparable cities was brainstormed, each member of the group was given five "weighted votes" as indicated on the list that follows. The weighted polling process made it clear to negotiators which of those characteristics should be used to determine comparable cities. That process is illustrated in Table 9.7.

A lengthy discussion of what factors might be included in selecting cities for the comparability study was averted because with a limited number of "votes" all members of the team gravitated to certain factors. All participants were able to quickly agree on a straw design suggesting that the study should be based on those factors that got a substantial number of marks: General population, the actual fire

Table 9.6   Instructions for Weighted Polling

1. Number all the items remaining on the list.

2. Give each member of the group between three and five "votes." Tell the participants they may distribute their selection as they wish, putting multiple votes on favorite items, **as long as they do not put all their marks on a single, favorite item.**

3. Collect the "votes" and tally the result. You may want to turn the chart away from the group, or wait to tally until everyone has selected their preferences, to prevent any members from being influenced by the pattern of early polling. Many groups use colored, "sticky dots" to provide a graphic tally of the results. Marks can also be placed on a separate chart listing the item numbers so as not to distract or influence members who are still deciding on their polling strategy.

4. Be sensitive to uneven balances in constituency representations "weighting" the vote in a way that is not intended. While this is rarely a problem in groups with a strong sense of team, it can be an issue if trust is low. An interesting way of "exploiting" such concerns to your advantage is to encourage each constituency group to use a different color, to give an instant indicator to the whole group of constituency sentiment.

5. Even at this stage, if anyone in the group feels strongly that an item should remain on the list for further discussion, that item should be retained. It is not unusual for an option that gets no initial marks to eventually be selected and implemented.

Table 9.7   Characteristics to Determine Comparable Cities

1. Comparable equipment*	9. Geographic proximity********
2. Overnight population*	10. Number of stations**
3. Daytime population	11. Revenue sources******
4. General population**********	12. Call volume***
5. Number of battalions	13. Number of firefighters
6. Fire services delivered******	14. Departments with paramedics***
7. # of high rise buildings**	15. City services delivered******
8. # of commercial buildings	16. Cost of housing**

functions that are performed by the department (suppression, prevention, training, and advanced life support), geographic proximity to the city being studied, sources of revenue supporting the cities, and the total number of overall services that the cities provide. It was agreed that these key criteria would deliver a good selection of similar cities, and a potentially divisive issue was quickly defused and decided.

The Matrix

When the list of options has been reduced to a manageable number, it is essential to have a focused discussion assessing the remaining options against the identified interests. The purpose of this process is to provide data to the group about the extent to which the options address the identified needs. This can involve a discussion that forces the group to prioritize interests. This is an important step at this point, because it raises the question of what is most important. It should be done as a team, and if there is disagreement, the interests should simply be placed at an equal ranking. The basic steps for the matrix tool are listed in Table 9.8.

Tools and Techniques

Table 9.8   Instructions for the Matrix

1. Prepare a chart as shown in Table 9.9, listing the options in abbreviated form down the left side, and core interests in the columns along the top of the page. Start with the highest priority interests in the first column and write across the chart from the most to the least important. This tool is best used when the interest and option lists have been reduced to a handful. It can be very unwieldy if there are too many of either.

2. Assess each option against each interest, using a number score, or a "High, Medium, or Low" rating to indicate the extent to which the option meets the interest. This should be done as a group discussion, rather than as individual "voting."

3. When the matrix is completed, you will have a good indication of which options hold the best possibility of reaching agreement by acceptably satisfying the most interests.

Sample Matrix

A coalition of leaders from several agencies and organizations needed to hire a consultant for a joint project. The group was having a difficult time selecting a candidate from a short list, partly because many members in the group had prior connections and loyalties to different candidates. After some consideration and consultation, they decided to use the matrix to structure their analysis and discussion.

Table 9.9   Which Consultant Should We Hire?

Options	Track record/results on similar projects	Interests, background, training, and consulting experience	Personality match with project team
Candidate #1	L	M	H
Candidate #2	H	H	M
Candidate #3	L	H	H

Although much of the initial lobbying was in favor of Candidates 1 and 3, Candidate 2 was ultimately selected, because the group was able to agree in advance that a personality match, while important, was less important than track record and technical skills. The matrix provided the group with a tool to analyze their options (the candidates) against their own predetermined criteria. While other criteria were also important, it was agreed that these three core interests were the overriding ones. The group hoped to complete this task in no more than 90 minutes, and thanks to the matrix the charge was completed on schedule.

THE STRAW DESIGN—JUST MAKE ONE!

A major focus of this book has been to think about leading in a way that draws a circle around the whole team. It is especially critical that the final stages of reaching an agreement stay consistent with this principle. Traditional negotiations (unfortunately) feature an *offer and acceptance* exchange of positions that separate stakeholders onto different pages, and the habit is very difficult to break. It seems harmless enough, but offer/counter-offer behaviors tend to bond stakeholders to their own proposals and to create a gap that is often impossible to bridge. Remember that we have worked hard to keep the stakeholders together as they generate options on a single list, so leaders must stay vigilant to keep their teams cooperating as they move toward agreement.

> *See Chapter 8 for a discussion of how groups can maintain a creative search for solutions and keep the team together on a single page.*

The straw design process has been adapted from sources that include the "one-text" mediation process described in *Getting To Yes* (Fisher & Ury, 1981, pp. 112–116). It is useful both in reducing the amount of time it takes the group to work through issues as well as in ensuring that agreement can be reached on complex problems. Of all the structuring tools that can be used to bring groups to agree-

> ***Tools and Techniques***

ment, this is the one that I tend to use almost every time I am trying to facilitate closure. The straw design is specifically designed to keep participants and their constituents working together on a single page, rather than factionalizing around separate proposals.

When the straw design process is used, the parties to problem solving work off the same page as a draft. Commitment is withheld by design until the very end of the process in order to keep group members from polarizing into positions before all creative possibilities have been explored and all the critical points have been covered. The model is a time saver because a few people can be empowered to draft solutions on behalf of the entire group, thus allowing everyone to work more efficiently. When drafts are returned, they belong to the whole group, so those creating them work at the pleasure of the larger group, avoiding attachment or ego involvement with the draft, which is expected to attract criticism by design. In this way, the individual or committee is appointed to draft a proposal that:

- Addresses the identified interests
- Conforms to any other identified guidelines of the group
- Incorporates any promising options brainstormed by the group, plus any other options that the author(s) feels might be helpful

When the draft is brought to the group for review the following rules listed in Table 9.10 are in force. Some groups like to use an old

Table 9.10   Instructions for the Straw Design

1. There is no ownership for the draft—it is made of "straw" and criticism cannot "hurt" it.

2. Criticism is welcome, but only with suggestions for how the "deficiencies" can be "fixed."

3. Participants are not asked to approve a draft until all other input has been exhausted.

4. The group should continue in a creative mode, searching for elegant ways of addressing the unmet needs.

5. If the group seems to be stuck, the conversation should focus on what it will take to make the concept acceptable to all the stakeholders.

6. Input is recorded, or submitted in writing, and the "author(s)" includes the feedback in the next draft.

7. This process continues, and the straw design is modified until there is no more criticism.

data processing model, in which the next versions are made of "wood," then "tin," and finally "iron." Each draft should become progressively tougher to criticize, and, although one school district budget-cutting process took almost 40 straw design iterations to produce agreement, many issues can typically be brought to closure in four versions or less. It is only at that point that negotiations are ended and the group is asked for consensus. If the straw plan does not produce consensus, the decision making process should revert to the agreed upon fallback method.

Beware of Making More Than One Straw Design

Old habits die hard, and even well-intentioned problem solvers can fall into those traps. Many leaders have experienced the problem that was reported by a principal who described how her staff came to an impasse when an attempt was made to reach agreement on a very critical issue.

Tools and Techniques

She summarized what had been done so far. "Everything seemed to be going just fine," she reported. "We clarified the task and the interests and came up with a great list of options. Then we broke into our separate groups to develop our straw designs, and they were really far apart!" Of course a huge piece of the problem could immediately be identified. The team inadvertently sent itself back to positional behavior by asking small groups to develop separate straw proposals on the same issue. Each group came back married to its own work, so the staff found itself unintentionally stalemated. Remember: The key feature of a straw design is that there is only one, and it is intended to address the needs of all participants. If coherence has been effectively created, a leader will be aware of the common ground, and will be able to help the group craft a proposal together that keeps them working on the same page, rather than on separate pages.

Crafting a Straw Design

An effective straw design will thus begin to address all of the critical needs of every key stakeholder. Because it remains a draft through the analysis phase, some license can be taken to try some components specifically designed to address the points of greatest friction that were described in Chapter 8 as significant obstacles to agreement. The crafters of a straw design need to have listened deeply to the interest-based conversation, including the evaluation of the options, to be able to devise a draft that allows all participants to see their own concerns reflected.

Tools and Techniques-Sample Straw Design

Table 9.11 shows the straw design that we developed in the meeting called to address the day labor issue described at the beginning of this chapter. Because the recommendations reflected in the design were to be submitted to staff, which expected to assume responsibility for implementation of any plan, the group's agreement could be more general in nature, trusting staff to fill in the details.

One of the issues keeping participants from agreeing to the concept of a center included the residents' desire to remove the disrupting influences of the day labor contracting from the residential area. But the day workers themselves expressed great concern that if the center were made too inaccessible to the local freeway, few contractors would find their way to the center to solicit their work. So maps were produced, and participants were able to find a general area that seemed to acceptably address everyone's needs related to location of the center.

Table 9.11   Design of a Day Labor Center

Participants recommend setting up a day labor center in partnership with a nonprofit agency and continuing education agency, with the following components:

1. Funding will be solicited by staff from various agencies, to be determined by staff.

2. Consumers, contractors, and related organizations will support the operation of the center.

3. Location of the center should be, if possible, within the area surrounded by S. Elm Street to the east, S. Airport Avenue to the west, Sixth Avenue to the north and E. Eleventh Avenue to the south, zoned as Central Business District-Support (CBD-S).

4. Day workers will be actively engaged in operations with paid administrator/staff, and a community oversight committee and partnership governing body.

5. Center should have operational policies to protect the rights of the workers.

6. Outreach to contractors and potential employers throughout the community needs to be conducted by center staff.

7. Center should include and/or be accessible to social services such as adult education, immigration education, medical services, and food services.

8. Law enforcement role and participation must be defined.

9. Center is established on a pilot basis for 18–24 months.

10. The potential nonprofit partner needs to have experience working with day labor population as well as interest in the day labor population.

11. Department staff will meet within the next several weeks to refine the straw design, brief the city manager on our efforts, and develop a next step plan to move this process forward. Copies of these minutes with the refined plan will be forwarded to all participants. The city manager and/or city council will take further responsibility for deploying this plan. Participants will be notified of any future meetings on this topic.

Similarly, some of the harshest critics of the center were troubled by the prospect that the day workers would exploit the citizens of the community for resources and income without sharing any ownership of the center operations, including the care and maintenance of the facility. Advocates for the workers were concerned about missing the opportunity to include essential health, educational, and immigration services in any center that is frequented by these workers. Almost everyone worried about the role that law enforcement would be playing in the operation. Provisions were included in the proposal listed in Table 9.11 to cover each of these concerns. Deep listening to the interests, and even the options that were discussed all morning long, led the group directly to a straw design that reflected everyone's needs acceptably. After a surprisingly brief conversation and a few modifications, it became clear that participants were ready to move toward closure, which they did by consensus. A year or two later, all their hard work became a reality, and the center was opened consistent with the plan.

PROPOSING CLOSURE

Chapter 1 included the story of a group I was observing that kept working at a task, although I had begun to "hear" an agreement sometime earlier in their discussion. When I finally interrupted to test my assumptions, it turned out that the group was, in fact, ready for closure. It is a critical leadership skill to learn to recognize when sufficient common ground has been identified in the development of solutions to suggest that the straw design is ready for closure. Propose it too late, and valuable time might be wasted and group members might become frustrated. Suggest it too soon, and the group might spiral into debate and argumentation.

Knowing when to push for agreement is often an intuitive process. Many well-intentioned groups are timid about proposing closure, and find themselves unable to make decisions because of this bashfulness. However, if proposing closure is either misused or overused, it can be destructive. Closure can be proposed according to the guidelines listed in Table 9.12.

Of course, the group's goal for closure in a consensus-oriented problem solving session is for all participants to show thumbs up or sideways. This tool is generally used only after there has already been substantial discussion on a subject and if proposal of closure seems appropriate. If a straw design has been created, it would generally have been

Tools and Techniques

thoroughly critiqued and improved before closure is proposed. The push toward closure must not come at the expense of valuable

Table 9.12   Instructions for Proposing Closure

1. When the parties appear ready to agree to a solution, test for consensus by recording the potential agreement for the group, and asking if everyone can accept or live with the decision. A "yes" from each participant means that a decision has been reached.

2. Remember that an issue important enough to need consensus probably needs a positive signal from every participant. This can be done with a simple "thumbs" signal to test agreement according to the same consensus definition that is listed in Table 9.2.

   ❑ **Thumbs up** means: "I am comfortable with this solution and can actively support it."

   ❑ **Thumbs sideways** means: "While I have reservations and this is probably not my preferred solution, I can live with it because we understand each other's points of view, the decision was reached openly and honestly, and my interests are acceptably addressed."

   ❑ **Thumbs down** means: "We have not had sufficient discussion, and do not yet understand one another's points of view. I have serious reservations and need more time to work on the issue." Or, "We understand each other, but this solution does not acceptably meet my interests. I cannot accept, support or, live with this approach."

dissent. It is important to set a tone where individuals will be willing to air sincerely held concerns, even if they reflect a minority perspective. People must know that such dissent is cherished, as a means of avoiding groupthink and that there will be no reprisals if they disagree with the majority.

See Chapter 4 for a discussion of groupthink and the dangers to coherence of suppressing dissent.

Remember that final closure should not be pushed until any key constituencies who are needed for a durable agreement can be involved in the decision. Ideally, representatives are checking back regularly to ensure that the constituents are up to speed on what is being considered, but straw designs will often need to be circulated to selected constituencies a number of times for input and critique. In one city where I had worked for some time to build problem-solving capacity, employees once complained that it seemed like the city manager and the city council were constantly undermining their work by overturning their proposed decisions. When pressed on the issue, they agreed that rather than abandoning their efforts to assume responsibility for problem solving, they needed to do a better job addressing the interests of those crucial constituents, and giving them ample opportunity to respond to how the straw design under consideration could be improved to better meet their needs.

Evaluating a Potential Solution

There are two critical criteria that should be used to evaluate any agreement before closure is proposed. First, the agreement should address all of the core interests acceptably, and the list reduction tools discussed earlier in this chapter are designed to facilitate such an analysis. A second very useful evaluation tool is the BATNA, which was described briefly (in Chapter 5) as the Best Alternative To A Negotiated Agreement. Each stakeholder may have his or her own unique BATNA, which is the fallback to an agreement, or what each party will do in the event that an agreement is *not* reached. There is real value in thinking about BATNA's in the context of the decision making, for they can help to protect against both making a bad agreement as well as passing up a good one.

We were able to reach agreement in that problem related to the contracting of day laborers because the BATNA for everyone was relatively unattractive. The problem was continuing to grow and it was clear that a law enforcement solution was not feasible, so most participants realized that if they could not solve the problem the status quo would most likely continue. The current situation was so unacceptable, that it increased everyone's motivation to find a mutually agreeable outcome. It often helps to name the BATNA when it can be done without a sense of threat or coercion, "We're all at this meeting because the day labor contracting in our community has begun to create some significant problems. It appears that our best hope for solving them is to work effectively together."

The Value of Saying "I Do"

I used to propose closure by asking if there was anyone in the group who could not live with the proposed decision. The problem with this approach is that it misses an opportunity for every member of the group to make an affirmative statement on behalf of the agreement. It also takes a good deal of courage to speak up when you may be one of the few holdouts, perhaps a little like the mythical wedding guest who has doubts about the match between the bride and groom actually saying something when asked to "speak now or forever hold your peace."

If everyone is asked for an affirmative sign of endorsement it requires every member of the group to take responsibility for the outcome and—more importantly—it allows problem solvers to scope out the areas that need improving. The reader may recall the elementary school mentioned in Chapters 1 and 3 that had been experiencing tremendous interpersonal conflict and needed a set of ground rules that would govern the meeting, as well as their future interactions. When we thought we had a list of acceptable ground rules we proposed closure, and much to the consternation of some participants, walked around the room looking for a signal from every person present indicating whether they could at least live with those rules. A half dozen of the participants had their thumbs down, or in their pockets, and so our conversation and work on the ground rules continued until everyone was comfortable with our plan. While some staff members were initially angry that we demanded a commitment, everyone was happy with the final product—one that improved the quality of their relationships for the long term.

GETTING IT ALL IN WRITING

When it is apparent that there is agreement, it must be polished to ensure that everyone has the same understanding of its terms and that it is likely to be fulfilled. An effective agreement will have clear details about the outcomes, including the *w*'s—*w*ho will do *w*hat, by *w*hen, and if appropriate, *w*here and ho*w*?

Tools and Techniques

Many a problem solver has left a meeting thinking ecstatically that an elegant agreement has been made, only to discover days, weeks, or months later that the agreement collapsed like a house of cards because no one followed through as they thought they had all committed. Often participants make assumptions about who will do what, and every member of the group walks out the door thinking that the deal is done and expecting someone else to take the lead. When no one does, people feel that there has been a betrayal, or at best that there has been a show of bad faith.

In fact, what there has been is a bad agreement. Make sure that there are explicit commitments *in writing* that clarify all the desired outcomes, including carefully thought-out deadlines. If a group will meet to plan or take the next action steps, spell out who will be the convener. Design provisions for reflection and team learning so that the group can come back together to evaluate how the plan went, and to change what needs fixing. If a group knows that there will be an opportunity to reflect on the progress of implementation, members can then relax about achieving that elusive perfection. I never stop marveling how educators who always encourage their students to learn from their mistakes have such a hard time cutting themselves the same slack. Make sure that every decision includes an opportunity for continuous improvement and you will multiply your chances for success accordingly. Table 9.13 provides a checklist for key characteristics of an agreement that is likely to be well implemented.

Table 9.13   Distinguishing Characteristics of an Effective Agreement

An effective agreement:

1. Is thorough and well conceived

2. Is understandable

3. Includes the "w's" (who, what, when, where . . .)

4. Includes a plan for communicating the agreement clearly

5. Includes a plan for obtaining and deploying appropriate resources (human, financial, equipment, etc.)

6. Includes any appropriate next steps

7. Includes provisions for piloting if necessary, and for reflection, learning, and evaluation

8. Plans for the optimal involvement of constituents

Implementation Planning

Detailed planning is an essential part of effective problem solving and decision making. Ownership of the planning, implementation, and evaluation process should be as collegial as the problem solving process itself. Implementation may be delegated to an individual or to a subgroup, but the whole group retains accountability for making sure that the plan is valid and doable. If others must approve the plan, which is so often the case, then a workable and viable plan can help to persuade the "approvers." The planning process itself also has the added benefit of testing the practicality of the decision and may result in changes to the agreement. Remember also that involving the people in the planning who will be involved in the implementation helps ensure ownership of the plan as well as smoother implementation.

Tools and Techniques

As mentioned earlier, thinking about the w's will help produce a thorough implementation plan. This includes ensuring that appropriate resources are available to accomplish the task. This planning might include some of the following key questions:

- What must be done? Identify major and secondary action steps.
- In what order should action be taken? Arrange action steps in the appropriate sequence.
- What equipment and materials, money, facilities, and human resources must be obtained and from where? Identify all the necessary resources for the plan, including where they will be obtained.
- Who must do what? Assign appropriate personnel to accomplish the tasks.
- When must actions be completed? Assign realistic due dates and some mechanisms to monitor the tasks.

The plan should also include actions that ensure communication to all who need to be informed. Check your assumptions about who needs to know about the decision. Communicate frequently during the implementation process to be certain that all concerned are aware of the progress. Errors of omission are common in the problem solving process and people of goodwill often find themselves in conflict as a result of mistaken assumptions.

Enter all these decisions onto a planning document, such as the one shown in Table 9.14.

The purpose of a planning document is to provide an archival record to the implementation and monitoring teams of exactly what the decision makers had in mind. The form of the document is less important than ensuring that the information has been efficiently captured to maximize the likelihood that the decision will be implemented as intended.

Table 9.14   Sample Implementation Worksheet

Major Activities	Responsibility	Sub-activities	Responsibility	Resources	When

The Gantt Chart

Another very useful tool for implementation planning is the Gantt Chart, which provides a graphic tool for documenting and summarizing the implementation plan. Each implementation activity is laid out in the Gantt Chart in the context of a calendar that shows how the implementation of each event interacts over time. A Gantt Chart is prepared by the following simple steps.

Tools and Techniques

1. Prepare a summary chart as shown in Table 9.15, with a column at the left of the chart for implementation activities and columns across the balance of the chart that detail the timelines that (depending on the project) may be in weeks, months, or quarters.

2. List the major action steps including activities related to implementation communication, monitoring, evaluation, and program improvement.

3. Draw a continuous horizontal line to indicate the scheduled beginning and endpoints of the activity.

Sample Gantt Chart

Table 9.15 displays the nonconstruction planning activities that will open a new elementary school. For illustrative purposes, these are the major activities that need to be accomplished. Each could be broken down into much more detailed planning steps and, depending on who is managing the project, may also include who is responsible for each step.

Monitoring, Evaluation, and Reflection

Don't overlook the importance of monitoring and evaluating progress. Even an implementation that seems to be going well may benefit from midcourse correction. Answer the following questions:

- What are the measurements of success?
- What are the milestones of achievement in the plan?
- Who will be responsible for monitoring and evaluating plan implementation?
- What are the pluses (that we want to continue) and the "delta's" (Greek symbol representing change) that we want to "fix" or do differently?

Table 9.15   Planning a New Elementary School

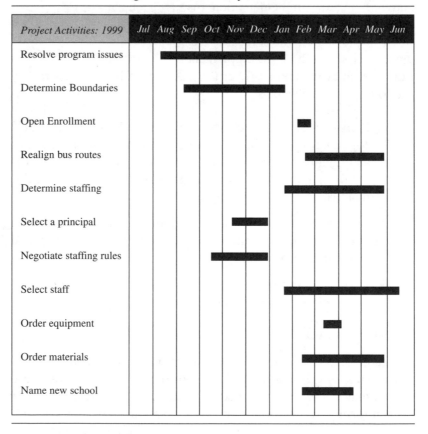

Project Activities: 1999	Jul	Aug	Sep	Oct	Nov	Dec	Jan	Feb	Mar	Apr	May	Jun
Resolve program issues		▬	▬	▬	▬	▬						
Determine Boundaries			▬	▬	▬	▬						
Open Enrollment								▬				
Realign bus routes								▬	▬	▬	▬	
Determine staffing							▬	▬	▬	▬		
Select a principal					▬							
Negotiate staffing rules				▬	▬							
Select staff							▬	▬	▬	▬	▬	
Order equipment									▬			
Order materials							▬	▬	▬			
Name new school							▬	▬				

If the solution required resource allocations, then there will be a need to generate data regarding its success in order to continue the allocation of potentially scarce resources. Pilot programs, for example, are easy targets for budget cuts if there is insufficient data to suggest their importance to the organization.

SUMMARY

An infrastructure for effective decision making should be in place long before a group ponders it's first difficult decision. Leaders who aspire to utilize consensus should be particularly thoughtful about how to organize a group or organization to ensure that it is poised to take advantage of coherence principles in order to produce excellent and efficient outcomes. This means developing the capacity of the entire group to stay on one page as they evaluate options against the key interests, to hear the common ground when it begins to coalesce, and to develop agreements that are likely to be honored and well implemented.

It has been the focus of this book to develop the capacity of leaders to work with the coherence principles to produce effective outcomes, and the last four chapters have detailed how to facilitate agreements from the point that the conversation begins through the validation of the final agreement. But there is always the tricky question of how to move from theory to practice. Chapter 10 considers how the reader can apply these attitudes and techniques to begin creating an organization that values, exploits, and perpetuates the principles of collaborative leadership.

CHAPTER TEN

Bringing Coherence to the Entire Organization

E fforts have been made in the preceding nine chapters to show the attitudes and the skills that combine to lead through collaboration. The unifying principles of coherence can be utilized in groups and organizations to allow participants to align their thinking and to produce outcomes and agreements that effectively meet everyone's needs. But how does a leader/practitioner who is intrigued by these concepts make the leap to implementation of the practices? How do we actually apply these aligning mechanisms to the messy mixture of people and institutions that are the reality of our day-to-day organizational lives? The purpose of this chapter is to show how formal or informal leaders can get started.

ALIGNING THE ORGANIZATION TAKES TIME

A few years ago, I began working with a couple dozen people who had come together to negotiate a labor agreement, each with their own unique perspectives on life, their own self-interests, their own distinctive philosophies on conflict, power, and leadership, and with a fractious collective history. As we politely assembled that first day, we looked around the table and could palpably feel the suspicion, mistrust, and anxiety that most of the participants brought along to the daunting task of addressing two decades of perceived economic inequities and adversarial interactions. But many of them also brought a sense of optimism and hopefulness that a spirit of collaboration and common purpose could replace the rancor of the past.

As the dialogue began, old wounds started to surface, and there were some heated exchanges, mostly related to assumptions about each other's intentions and ability to truly replace coercive power with a spirit of collaboration. However, some participants were new to the process, and no other approach made any sense to them. "Of course we can do this," they asserted. "Let's get to work."

We carefully structured the tasks and our activities to ensure that there were some deep conversations about interests and intentions, and options were generated to find ways to resolve the problems. While there were numerous missteps along the way, what unfolded over the months was a gradual alignment in thinking about what participants hoped to accomplish in the bargain and how they could make that dream a reality. While they came to the sessions with a clear sense of advocacy for their constituencies, at least for that period of time they also began to see themselves as one team. And this sense of common purpose, patience, and commitment seemed to lead them inevitably to outcomes that all could embrace much more easily than either side could have accomplished on its own.

Letting Go of the Quick Fix

When viewed over time and compared to the suspicions and hostility they had initially brought with them into the room, the coherence that this group created was remarkable. But measured from one meeting to the next, it sometimes looked as if they were going nowhere, and very possibly making things worse. It takes time to lead by consensus, just as it takes time to reach it, and it is critical for a leader to understand this concept and not to expect a quick fix where a long-term endeavor is in order. Although many of the tools and attitudes that have been presented in this book will help a conflicted group extricate itself from an ongoing fiasco, the best time to think about leading by consensus is long before the group begins the problem-solving process. This suggests the value of a "planful" approach to creating coherence.

Planning for Change

Table 10.1 contains a checklist for leading by consensus comprising the elements of a "next steps" plan. Thoughtful attention to

Table 10.1   A Checklist for Leading by Consensus

1. Demonstrate leadership commitment

2. Develop a vision and keep it in focus

3. Attend to relationships

4. Maintain open and collaborative communications and problem-solving mechanisms

5. Structure the organization to deliver what is promised

6. Remain mindful of the learning

---

each of these planning elements will not only provide clues to the best place to start, but will also help to ensure that systems issues get identified and addressed in the process. Each of these key elements provides an entry point that will help to align the organization more effectively. The creation of an organization that can make great decisions with a high degree of ownership can be advanced if each of these elements is thoughtfully addressed.

DEMONSTRATE LEADERSHIP COMMITMENT

There is perhaps no factor that can have a more powerful impact on the ability of an organization or team to assume collaborative approaches, than for the key leaders to continually demonstrate their commitment to the process. That commitment requires a delicate balance between a vigilant focus on the business of the organization and thoughtful attention to the needs of the people who are getting the business done. Team members will be continually and cautiously watching the leaders to verify that they are serious about the "people part" of consensus, as well as engrossed in the business at hand.

Thinking About Power

This phenomenon is particularly prevalent in labor relationships, which are often very adversarial. When efforts to create coherence in a labor relationship fail, it is often connected to an inability or

Table 10.2   Power Sources

PERSONAL POWER	*VESTED POWER*
Defined by Relationship **Characterized by:** • Trustworthiness • Dependability • Collegiality • Responsibility • Humility	**Defined by Authority** **Characterized by:** • Position • Status • Autonomy • Coercive alternatives • Superiority
Leadership Through Commitment: • Problem solving • Flat organization • De-emphasized hierarchy • Shared authority	**Leadership Through Control:** • Positional authority • Layered and top-down • Status symbols • Sole authority

unwillingness by leaders to give up traditional sources of power in the relationship. Table 10.2, which is based on the work of John Kotter (1985), lists alternative sources of power in an organization. Both must be appropriately "wielded" and a leader needs to be mindful of when and how either might be used. Vested power is based on the institutional authority that a leader commands. For example, in a labor relationship, management leaders have the right to unilateral implementation and control over the organization's resources and labor leaders have the capacity to mobilize union members in unilateral sanctions through job actions. The grievance process is created as a formal mechanism for addressing problems, and it tends to be used as a control mechanism.

Collaborative leadership clearly falls on the "personal" side of the chart, and the tools and attitudes in this book are intended to maximize the effectiveness of a leader aspiring to operate out of personal power. This is particularly important in situations in which a person is striving to influence groups or individuals who are more powerful than he or she is in the formal organizational hierarchy. With little organizational control over superiors they can only really be influenced through personal power.

Two very similar school districts model the tension between these two power sources. Both are sizable districts that were experiencing animosity in the labor-management relationship, and in each case the union and management leaders understood that their own negative interactions were contributing to the toxicity. In both cases the leaders got together to determine how the relationships could be improved. Each set of leaders had honest conversations with plenty of blunt feedback about the behaviors that were promoting adversarialism.

In one district, each leader owned the personal behavior that was contributing to the dysfunction and committed to changes that would model the desired collaboration for the rest of the organization. With this mutual resolve in place, and the appropriate communication mechanisms to solve problems as quickly as they appeared, the relationship prospered and they reached mutually acceptable agreements in extremely difficult financial circumstances. In the other organization the leaders continued to blame the dysfunction on each other and to wait for the others to take the first unilateral step toward improving the relationship. Of course no one did, and as a result the toxic relationships continued and worsened. Whereas one relationship reprogrammed their future to become collaborative and mutually beneficial, the other resigned itself to adversarial interactions that worsened the mistrust and compromised the organization's ability to address its core mission.

Three Critical Questions

Although labor-management relations magnify the power issues, almost any organization, including a family, needs to wrestle with how power is exercised. Remembering that we can never really abdicate our vested power, we must make a conscious decision to increase our capacity to practice personal power. In this regard, I have found that there are three critical questions that really resonate with groups that are struggling with their own relationships. They are listed in Table 10.3. When the formal and informal leaders of an organization honestly reflect together on these questions, they can generally determine whether they have the individual and collective will to actually lead the group through collaboration. Often, as in the case of the two labor relationships described above, individuals are afraid to answer "yes" to the three questions, and so an honest inquiry is needed to figure out what it will take to adequately address those fears so that leaders and other group members will give up the use of positional power as a first resort. This involves an expressed

Table 10.3   Three Critical Questions

1. Am I (are we) genuinely committed to partnering in the relationship?

2. Do I (do we) believe "they" are genuinely committed to partnering?

3. Am I (are we) willing to make partnering our conflict resolution method of first resort?

desire and commitment from all parties to change the relationship. When participation is voluntary and mutual, then the more proactive change agents will generally draw others along with their enthusiasm and positive experiences. Sometimes this also needs to include asking group members to acknowledge that not changing will result in more of the status quo, which is often unattractive or unacceptable. Understanding the negative consequences that will result from *not changing* the relationship can serve as a motivator to move the relationship to a better place.

Learning to Embrace Imperfection

It should be clear that leading by consensus means acknowledging our own need to change. Remember from Figure 3.4 that the path from discord to generative engagement runs through introspection and reframing. The process of leadership is messy, and accepting one's own fallibility allows a leader to serve as the "learner in chief" and willingly open the doors and windows to the honest input of others inside and outside of the organization. When we introduced a 360-degree feedback process to our organization, leaders unaccustomed to hearing others comment on their shortcomings greeted it with some genuine and understandable apprehension. But the conversations that it produced about how to improve leadership and learning were generally perceived to be exhilarating and productive because of their potential for advancing the way business is done. What it requires is openness to feedback, willingness of managers to embrace their own imperfection, and commitment to consensus-oriented leadership.

"Walking the Talk"

The burden is also on leaders to model the tools and attitudes that will create coherence and help groups reach agreements more effectively. We have discussed how our habit-based behavior tends to program us to do business in the same old ways. It takes more work to use structuring tools to organize the conversation in a meeting, including the use of interest analysis and options generation to lead problem solving. But the tools and techniques that are described in Chapters 5 through 9 of this book will help a group to conduct a conversation in a way that it will align itself around a collaborative agreement. This means that leaders must have the conscious discipline to push a group to think deeply about interests before it jumps to a solution, and to listen carefully for the common ground so that agreements can be named as they begin to be formulated.

When leaders ask their teams to become skillful in problem-solving approaches, those team members will notice when those skills are modeled and when they are not. Chapters 3 and 4 include some examples from one city that has deeply embraced the coherence principles. In this case the city manager considers consensus-based leadership and civic engagement to be at the heart of his approach to public leadership, and so every important issue is framed throughout the organization and the community, including the city council, in terms of the interests and options involved. His relentless focus on coherence principles is a visible reminder to citizens and employees alike that there is an expectation that inquiry and problem solving are at the heart of how business is done in the city, and they see and hear it modeled by the city manager on a daily basis.

Identify the Leadership Team

If there is not already a natural leadership team in the group or organization, then one should be developed. The team should have natural connections to the rest of the organization, and will become what Kotter (1996) calls a "guiding coalition" to take responsibility for creating and perpetuating the organizational vision. Although one charismatic leader may be able to mold an organization in her image and single-handedly hold it for the period of her tenure, deeper and longer lasting change requires the organization to maintain the vision at a much broader level. DuFour and Eaker (1998) characterize a "professional learning community [as] a group of collaborative teams that share a common purpose" (p. 26). Small school and departmental groupings can serve as a leadership team, but larger organizations will require a guiding coalition to take responsibility for perpetuating the vision.

A vision that is based on coherence requires a similar guiding coalition of formal and informal leaders willing to put themselves out as a model for cooperation and collaboration. I have seen public sector leadership teams made up of a wide variety of members, from city council members, custodians, electricians, bus drivers, parents, teachers, chief executives, and community members. The only requirement is recognition of the value of collaboration to the achievement of the organization's vision, and a commitment to publicly modeling the desired behaviors and a willingness to facilitate the coherence process including a relentless inquiry into ways of improving things.

DEVELOP A VISION AND KEEP IT IN FOCUS

In Chapters 5 and 7 we consider the importance of vision and interests to collaborative leadership. Any reader who is attracted to the approaches described in this book most likely already has a vision that is coherent with these principles, but conversations will need to be held throughout the organization to be certain that the values are widely shared and that there is a readiness for consensus-oriented approaches. For obvious reasons, it is hugely problematic to attempt to autocratically mandate collaboration.

Understanding the Reasons for Collaborating

A leader aspiring to introduce coherence principles to an organization should be clear on why collaborative approaches will add value to the organization. Although we live in a world that most assuredly can benefit from kinder and gentler interaction, that is generally not an adequate reason for devoting organizational resources to collaboration. Leaders must be convinced that it will produce better results and there needs to be a perceived fit between the organizational mission and how business is conducted from day-to-day. Leaders also need to communicate that fit throughout the organization.

For example, many school districts are turning to alternative dispute resolution practices to resolve disagreements between parents and districts over the individualized educational plans for students with special needs. The unnecessary expense that is incurred in mediations and due process hearings and the animosity that is created between families and school districts is ample reason to strive for a collaborative approach. But there must also be a vision within the organization that sees the students served best by a partnership between regular and special education teachers and parents to deliver instructional services that address the unique needs of every learner. This will cause the entire organization, including parent advocates, to become well situated for problem solving and for differentiating and optimizing the educational program for every student. Public sector organizations are in the business of community building and creating the future, and so it is important to give thought to how human interaction reflects that mission.

This does not mean that an organization's vision should be solely focused on collaboration. DuFour and Eaker (1998) assert that vision "instills an organization with a sense of direction" (p. 62), and so it must be shown how coherence principles will enhance the core work. My own district's vision asserts that we will collaborate throughout the organization, district, school staff, students, parents, and community to ensure that students master or exceed their standard expectations or individual goals and that they do it in a way that maintains and instills a passion for learning. We recognize in our vision that the high-stakes expectations that our society is placing on education are so complex that it is *only* through collaboration that we can be successful. In this particular organization we appreciate the role that consensus approaches need to play, and we struggle on a daily basis to try to figure out how to put them into practice in the context of our instructional focus.

Staying Mindful of the Vision

It is the task of the guiding coalition of leaders to keep the focus on what is most important. It is critical to avoid becoming so absorbed in the day-to-day operational problems that the vision gets lost. When operational problems do become distractions, leaders must find ways to methodically and relentlessly refocus on the strategic vision if it is to become a reality. When my own school district limped to the conclusion of an unexpectedly bitter labor negotiation in 1985, the agreement had not even been formally ratified when farsighted voices on the school board assembled union and management leaders to refocus on the interests and values that would eventually reset the stage for many years of uninterrupted labor-management collaboration.

Leaders should be continually prioritizing their own interests and those of the organization, the leadership team, and key constituents and stakeholders. There should be little doubt about what the organization should be doing, so that members feel empowered to pursue the vision and do what is right without needing to be directed. Business and organizational literature is filled with testimonials to what many consider to be a quintessential example of organizational focus. During the product tampering scare in the early 1980s involving cyanide-laced capsules of Tylenol, Johnson & Johnson acted within hours to remove the product from shelves and to withhold the product from the market worldwide, until it could be demonstrated to be safe. There was clear coherence throughout the company around the need for absolute product integrity, and that alignment enabled people at all levels to act in a way that held the long-term vision sacredly above interests in short-term profit or avoiding blame.

ATTEND TO RELATIONSHIPS

Consensus-based approaches are exploited by carefully allowing people to have conversations that create coherence in their thinking and that, in the process, illuminate the common ground between them. This requires very careful attention to the people and their relationships, and so a leader must concentrate on relationships as well as the task. Remember from Chapter 6 that every problem has a content, process, and relationship component, and by habit most of us go straight to the content and forget about the rest. It is especially easy to overlook the relationship, which is often a messy and uncomfortable arena for program improvement.

Returning to the Relationship

A leader aspiring to embed these principles in the team must take steps at the outset to focus on relationships. This means making provisions for a thoughtful process in which the parties can share perceptions about how they interact and establish mutual goals and an agenda for improving relations. Whether or not there is antagonism among the parties, the story should be told with an opportunity for each key stakeholder or group to acknowledge the perception of the others and to hear their own perspectives recognized and understood. I try to do this regularly with teams on which I play a key role, and it is a practice that seems to be gaining in popularity as schools and departments throughout our organization are increasingly scheduling sessions to consider how working relationships can be enhanced in order to improve instruction.

There are a variety of "rubs" that may be identified in this process, but generally they involve noticing how habit-based behavior can compromise the team's efforts to implement their vision. Following are some examples of the kinds of issues that have surfaced in teams that mindfully focus on relationships. Almost every case gets resolved well by understanding the role that relationships play in conflict, and by developing agreements or crafting norms to resolve the problematic behavior.

- A nonprofit agency team that was geographically distributed was experiencing some communications difficulties that were causing key members to be left out of the loop, thus adversely impacting the productivity of the organization. Agreements were made to ensure that all participants were included in key decisions, accessed communications in a timely manner, and made commitments that were clear, specific, and compliance-prone.

- A school leadership team recognized that they were permitting staff members to engage in personal attacks that were destroying trust, undermining morale, and preventing staff members from working together effectively to improve instruction. They agreed—as a team—to take a stand against the behavior by naming the attacks as they were occurring and to make it clear to all colleagues that such conduct would no longer be tolerated.

- The senior managers in a hospital realized that an adversarial relationship had been created between the hospital and the doctors who were their primary providers. They set out to find ways to maximize their ability to partner with the physicians on economic and quality of care issues.

Even though these outcomes are really just examples of continuous improvement processes at work, it is critical for leaders to be vigilant to the fact that relationship issues significantly impede organizational effectiveness, so they must be faithfully monitored and courageously addressed if an organization is to be effective. Every team needs to have agreements that will ensure that people problems are identified and resolved in a timely manner, long before they become the proverbial "elephants in the parlor" that everyone sees, but nobody addresses, and that make it impossible for the organization, group, or family to function effectively.

Make Sure That Norms Are in Place

This also means acknowledging from the outset that mistakes will occur and giving permission for anyone to admit that a mistake has been made and to rectify it without losing face. It also means establishing communications mechanisms to ensure a principled relationship, with individual and group accountability for commitments to change. These things are best accomplished by creating norms that make explicit the behaviors that will be needed to guide the conduct of individual group members and for the relationship to function effectively. Effective norms are an important prerequisite for a well-aligned group, and it is one of the first things that should be introduced in the process.

See Chapter 6 for information on how to create norms.

Thinking About "Customers"

An organization is a system, and when it is healthy and thriving, all the parts will be in alignment, working together for the greater good. In most organizations in today's complex environment, that alignment must be extended well beyond the policy setters to include the staff that do the work of the organization, as well as the clients who receive the services and whose satisfaction is critical to everyone's success, particularly in public sector organizations in which the customers are also the "owners."

Most everyone in the twenty-first century workplace is a customer, whether it is someone "across the counter" whose patronage is the life's blood of the organization, another department, a supervisor, or a subordinate whose success in the organization is inextricably linked to our own. A well-aligned organization necessarily requires a deep understanding of the needs of all the stakeholders.

Frequently a hostile patron is really a disgruntled customer who feels that the "bureaucrats" are insensitive to his or her needs. The skills of inquiry and advocacy introduced in prior chapters are particularly useful in ensuring that everyone at least feels understood, and has a reasonable expectation that their interests are being taken into account.

This by no means implies that all that is required to transform a hostile customer into a supportive team member is a little inquiry. Certainly there are numerous instances in which customers will leave dissatisfied, whether their dissatisfaction is due to the organization's inability or unwillingness to satisfy them, or because of customers' own emotionalism or irrationality. But I have learned over the years that a sympathetic ear and a willingness to understand the point of view behind a complaint can break down barriers and inform the system. In one case, a mother and daughter came to see me to appeal the way the daughter had been "thrown out" of school. What they seemed to need most from me was not my agreement with their perspective, but rather understanding and acknowledgement of that point of view. ("I can see why it feels to you that we let you and your daughter down.") In this case, the daughter was already 18 years old and enrolled in the adult school. What the mom really wanted was for the system to learn from all of our collective shortcomings related to her daughter, including her own mistakes. When she felt that I understood her problem and would take steps to see how the system could be improved to learn from the experience, she was able to walk out of my office feeling part of the team.

Partnering Throughout the Organization

Over the years I have encountered some educators who see parents either as antagonists not to be trusted or as lackeys needing to be directed. But of course the reality is that parents are the educators who have the greatest influence on the success of the student. For a school to ignore the vital role they play on the team is to eliminate the support system most able to make a difference. In some cases, that means figuring out how to win back a team member who for a variety of reasons may have long ago defected from the educational relationship. The very same principle applies to other public sector organizations, which need to find ways of partnering with the citizens they are striving to serve. For this reason, many cities are turning to community design review as a way of giving neighborhoods significantly more ownership in projects that are planned in their area. While it may be difficult to please everyone, it is much easier to build ownership when there is early involvement in the project design phases.

Similarly, it is critical to align partnerships among staff in an organization. This involves cultivating personal power to the extent that hierarchical relationships are subordinated to problem-solving relationships. A collaborative leader must by definition demonstrate a commitment to inclusion. For me this involves a personal commitment to treat a phone call from a principal, a union leader, a staff member, or a parent with at least the attention that I would give a call from a school board member. I also believe that it means thinking of ways to organize a school district central office as a consulting firm that regards the rest of the organization as its valued customers and places customer effectiveness and satisfaction as two of its highest goals.

Thus leading through collaboration is a way of engaging the whole organization in the process of leadership. In the preface I named the assumption that a leader is "anyone with the motivation, honesty, and courage to describe, without blame, the problems or situations that need to be changed, and to put in motion a search for better ways of doing things." In order to make the most of this cadre of change agents, a leader who does have positional power should organize things in a way that makes it clear that such leadership is encouraged. In this way everyone needs to think differently about leadership. For example, Dee Hock (1999), founder of Visa, which was conceived and based on nonhierarchical organizational principles, asserts that an effective manager is responsible for leading oneself, one's superiors, and one's peers before thinking about leading subordinates (pp. 68–73). An organization that encourages its leaders to take responsibility for themselves and to put their energy and initiative into influencing their peers and superiors will be an organization that solves problems effectively and achieves a high level of positive coherence.

Effective Constituency Relationships

A constituency is a group of people who are served by an organization and, accordingly, anyone who aspires to lead with a significant level of consensus needs to involve constituencies early in the process. For example, a teachers association was able to build a very long-lasting labor relationship with the school district by including their suspicious constituents in the decision to get started. They wrote a series of fliers detailing the successes that had been gained from "hard bargaining" and the costs that adversarial relations had extracted. They also conducted a series of meetings in the schools and eventually held a referendum to determine whether the association members supported a collaborative effort. It was overwhelmingly approved, and the relationship enjoyed strong support from the rank-and-file members.

By contrast, leaders who try to improve labor relationships without carefully including the members in the process often find that their efforts are regarded with suspicion and mistrust. One city, which had developed positive relationships with each of their unions, discovered that their hard

> ### *Tools and Techniques*

work was undermined by a city council that didn't understand or own the relationship or the interests; thus they failed to ratify the agreements that had been painstakingly and collaboratively negotiated. Another city in which there were unsuccessful efforts to mediate an agreement between grocery store developers and citizens who opposed the store, learned in retrospect that failure to include the citizens who favored a new store left the mistaken impression that the conflict pitted the developers against the entire community.

In general, constituencies become alienated when they feel like they are out of the loop. All of the principles of openness apply, and so excellent communication mechanisms should be developed with frequent checking to ensure that the assumptions leaders are making about stakeholder interests are accurate, and that there are ongoing opportunities for input and reflection on how the organization's efforts can be improved to better meet their needs. This may not require the creation of new institutions, but it will involve making efforts to maximize the input from community conferences, commissions, advisory committees, and site councils in addition to providing ample information for an informed dialogue. This also involves identifying key people, including leaders, subgroups, and opinion makers throughout the organization whose ownership will assist the effort or who are likely to take an interest. Training may be useful to demystify the inquiry and problem solving skills that will be practiced throughout the organization, and to broaden the base of future leaders who will be needed to continue these cultural changes.

MAINTAIN OPEN AND COLLABORATIVE COMMUNICATIONS AND PROBLEM-SOLVING MECHANISMS

This book has focused in detail on both the attitudes and skills that are necessary for leading through collaboration. Both are necessary for successful implementation, and so leaders must—at the outset— begin looking for places to embed collaborative practices, not only so they will be visible to constituents but also because collaborative attitudes will not last long if the work is still being done by closed and competitive systems. Leaders will need to audit their organizations to find the places where open communications and problem-solving approaches can take hold and prove their value to the whole organization.

Table 10.4 presents a starter list of areas that are prime places to begin implementing a vision of coherence. Members of the organization need to begin talking together about how best to begin that

Table 10.4   Areas for Leading Through Collaboration in an Organization

1. Leadership Meetings

2. Governance Meetings

3. Public Hearings

4. Media Relations

5. Labor Relations

6. Public Relations

7. Internal and External Communications Systems

8. Professional Development Programs

9. Human Resource Systems

10. Organizational Policies

11. Complaint Policies

12. Budget Development

process in any given area. I know in my own professional life that I need to continually remind myself of the vision and practice it regularly in each of these areas. I feel like I am most successful when I go out of my way to ensure that meetings are thoughtfully structured to maximize problem solving or when I make certain that I am communicating openly, early, and often. When I neglect these practices or (for whatever reason) choose not to use them I am far more likely to be frustrated or disappointed with the outcome, and so are my constituents and colleagues.

Every organization will have its own priorities for where to begin collaborative efforts. The human resource department is ripe with opportunities, from the hiring process to employee evaluation and discipline. There are numerous personnel applications in which problem-solving approaches can vault the organization toward greater collaboration. Much has been said in these pages of the application of these tools to labor relationships, and union and management leaders should begin talking as early as possible about how to reorganize their interactions to produce better outcomes. Meetings at all levels of the organization should be analyzed for how collaborative practices can improve productivity and feeling tone. Problem solving skills should be introduced and modeled and—anywhere possible— meetings should be systematically organized with appropriate structuring tools. When a problem solving vocabulary (like "interests" or "options") is introduced and appropriately charted in all meetings the process gains credibility and the members of the organization gain confidence that there is a "method to the madness."

Defining Success

Having analyzed where to begin, choose carefully from the possibilities according to readiness in the organization. As Kotter (1996) advises, look for "short-term wins" (pp. 117–130). Define in advance what changes will indicate that the new approach has been successful, and acknowledge the progress to one another at every step along the way. If the change involves a department or work team, "top" management should remain in touch with the undertaking and continue to offer support. Similarly, take small but recognizable steps to build trust, especially if the approaches are being applied to a traditionally adversarial relationship. Strategize together what a higher level of trust ought to look like and sound like.

Define what new structures will look like once the process has been implemented. This can include some of the following considerations:

- How will meetings be managed? Who will fill the structural roles of facilitator and recorder?
- If the change involves economic or other difficult negotiations with unions, customers, venders, or developers, what unique standards, processes, and techniques will be used to address financial issues to prevent positionalism?

> *See Chapter 8 for more on standards and other techniques for generating options on divisive issues.*

- What problem-solving methods will be used to identify and address ongoing issues, and what will happen when the parties disagree?
- What roles will key constituents play?
- What traditional problem-solving practices need to be changed? Presuming that people fall back on what is familiar, what practices would be the most destructive if they reappeared out of habit? What can be done to ensure that they are permanently replaced by new habits?

STRUCTURE THE ORGANIZATION TO DELIVER WHAT IS PROMISED

In the spirit of form following function, consideration should be given in the planning stages to arranging the organization in a way that supports the values that are being advanced through the vision. One sanitation district that wanted to incorporate collaborative leadership throughout the organization, eliminated a whole level of hierarchy by turning their supervisors into coaches. They found that they still needed to reprogram old hierarchical habits on the part of both the coaches and the employees, but their organizational changes gave them a significant advantage compared to similar entities that tried to change behaviors without addressing their hierarchical structures. Similarly, our school district leadership team wanted to offer more support and less directives to schools, and so created a "learning support partner" role in which every central office certificated manager supports a cluster of schools to focus on student achievement as well as to offer other problem-solving support.

It will take a considerable amount of time and effort to make these changes successful, but an organizational design that hasn't been planned to deliver the change that is envisioned may not be capable of delivering what is most wanted. That being said, such changes should be made carefully and thoughtfully, avoiding the "flavor of the month" that offers the latest fad that may be incompatible with what the organization most needs. Argyris (2000) cautions that a "good choice . . . is one made consciously and one based on valid data and sound reasoning" (p. 192).

> *The tools shared in Chapters 6 through 9 also apply to conceiving and implementing an approach to leadership.*

Careful attention should be given to the interests that must be satisfied by any leadership approach and to the specific circumstances of the organization. Care should also be taken to plan and implement a change strategy that meets the needs of the organization and its members, and consideration should be given to ensure ongoing reflection and learning.

REMAIN MINDFUL OF THE LEARNING

It may be impossible to separate effective leadership from effective learning. I think back many years to an experience of my own related to powerful teaching and learning, and it has some compelling implications for leadership. I was among a group of adults from a variety of public and nonprofit agencies who were enrolled together in a leadership course in a wilderness setting in the Boundary Waters Canoe Area of Northern Minnesota. We were canoe trekking and had spent some time learning navigation methods as well as perfecting our paddling and expedition techniques. In the spirit of wilderness learning, once it had been determined that our skill level was acceptable, our instructor became silent and turned over control of the voyage to the students. We made some amazing blunders, and ended up paddling two days out of our way before we realized what had happened, found our bearings, and headed back to our intended ending place. Our instructor attended to our safety, the most critical interest any of us brought to the enterprise, and left us entirely in charge of the rest of the learning around leadership. In the course of the adventure, we learned self-sufficiency in an extreme environment, teamwork, and how to move beyond failure. We also eventually learned how to work very effectively together to discover when we were off course, to assess what was wrong and to determine how to fix it. We became proficient at a task that was alien to most of us. Most assuredly our instructor learned from our mistakes as well and became a better teacher and leader because of them.

This experience is a great metaphor for leadership. What is required is a deep understanding that learning is really at the heart of organizational growth and alignment. Effective change agents apply these learning principles to the enterprise of leading. For example, a principal with a sense of where a school needs to be in order to be successful should have the patience and the wisdom to allow staff and parents to collectively determine how to get there. A new fire chief must understand that his or her conflict-torn department needs the chief to listen first and appreciate the sources of upheaval that have filled their working lives for years and then give them the permission and hold them accountable to change the relationships that were impeding their effectiveness. A university department head will recognize the passion and the vision of the members of the department and empower them to reconceive the very nature of the way business is done to ensure that an already successful program keeps pace with the changing needs of its client base. Most importantly, a team member will have the clarity and the courage to identify and name the behaviors and circumstances that are perceived to be hampering the team's effectiveness.

Leaders mindfully prepare the organization for the aligning principles that will allow coherence to be created. They ensure that the organization has a vision consistent with its goals and mission, and that the members of the group have the conversations that are needed to figure out how to get there. They empower their teams to act, and when a problem is detected, they prod group members to work together to figure out the cause and how it should be addressed. They listen thoughtfully to understand the common ground and to make certain that what is being considered and how it is being organized are both consistent with the vision of the team. They attend to the relationships and force group members to deal with the difficult topics that must be considered to keep the vision flourishing. They are the "Learners in Chief" who model reframing by openly inquiring into how their own behavior might be contributing to a problem and by willingly making the changes that are needed to improve.

By thoughtfully aligning the team, leaders can harness self-organizing principles to advance the effectiveness of the organization. Perhaps there may be some greater benefit to our efforts to achieve coherence at home and in the workplace. If more of us begin to think mindfully about how we lead our lives and how we interact with others when we respond to conflict, then we may begin to diminish the impact of the flight-or-fight responses that are so prevalent and so dangerous in human relationships. It all begins at home and with oneself. It is not about finding new strategies for changing others, but using the natural energy of coherence to support one another as we develop an inner capacity to change ourselves.

References

Argyris, C. (1993). *Knowledge for action: A guide to overcoming barriers to organizational change*. San Francisco: Jossey-Bass.

Argyris, C. (2000). *Flawed advice and the management trap: How managers can know when they're getting good advice and when they're not*. New York: Oxford University Press.

Argyris, C., & Schon, D. A. (1974). *Theory in practice*. San Francisco: Jossey-Bass.

Bohm, D. (1980). *Wholeness and the implicate order*. London: ARK.

Bohm, D. (1990). *On dialogue*. Ojai, CA: David Bohm Seminars.

Bunker, B. B., & Alban, B. T. (1997). *Large group interventions: Engaging the whole system for rapid change*. San Francisco: Jossey-Bass.

Byron, G. G. (1904). The prisoner of Chillon. In *Byron: Poetical Works*. London: Oxford University Press. (Original work published 1816.)

Collins, J. (2001). *Good to great: Why some companies make the leap . . . and others don't*. New York: HarperCollins.

Columbia Accident Investigation Board. (2003). *Report of Columbia Accident Investigation Board*. National Aeronautics and Space Administration and the Government Printing Office. Available http://www.nasa.gov/columbia/home/CAIB_Vol1.html

de Chardin, P. T. (1955). *Building the earth*. Wilkes-Barre: Dimension Books.

de Chardin, P. T. (1959). *The phenomenon of man*. New York: Harper and Row.

de Tocqueville, A. (2000). *Democracy in America*. In H. C. Mansfield & D. Winthrop (Ed., Trans., & Intro), *Democracy in America*. Chicago: University of Chicago Press. (Original work published in 1835.)

Dickmann, M. H., & Stanford-Blair, N. (2002). *Connecting leadership to the brain*. Thousand Oaks, CA: Corwin Press.

Dobson, C., Hardy, M., Heyes, S., Humphreys, A., & Humphreys, P. (1981). *Understanding psychology*. London: Weidenfeld and Nicholson.

DuFour, R., & Eaker, R. (1998). *Professional learning communities at work: Best practices for enhancing student achievement*. Bloomington, IN: National Educational Service.

Ellinor, L., & Gerard, G. (1998). *Dialogue: Rediscover the transforming power of conversation*. New York: John Wiley & Sons, Inc.

Fisher, R., & Ury, W. (1981). *Getting to yes: Negotiating agreement without giving in*. New York: Penguin.

Follett, M. P. (1940). Constructive conflict. In Metcalf, H. C., & Urwick, L. (Eds.), *Dynamic administration: The collected papers of Mary Parker Follett*. New York and London: Harper.

Fritz, R. (1991). *Creating*. New York: Ballantine Books.

Fullan, M. (2001). *Leading in a culture of change*. San Francisco: Jossey-Bass.

Fullan, M. (2003). *The moral imperative of school leadership*. Thousand Oaks, California: Corwin Press.

Gendlin, E. T. (1978). *Focusing*. New York: Everest House.

Gladwell, M. (2000). *The tipping point: How little things can make a big difference*. Boston: Little, Brown and Company.

Glaser, J. P. (2001). Walking the talk: Collaborating and thriving in an adversarial culture. *International Electronic Journal for Leadership in Learning, 5*(1). Available from http://www.ucalgary.ca/~iejll/volume5/glaser.html

Gleik, J. (1987). *Chaos: Making a new science*. New York: Penguin Books.

Goldhagen, D. J. (1996). *Hitler's willing executioners: Ordinary Germans and the holocaust*. New York: Knopf.

Goswami, A. (2000). *The visionary window: A quantum physicist's guide to enlightenment*. Wheaton, IL: Quest Books.

Griffin, E. (1997). *A first look at communication theory*. New York: McGraw-Hill.

Hargrove, R. (1995). *Masterful coaching: Extraordinary results by transforming people and the way they think and work together*. San Francisco: Jossey-Bass.

Hauptman, O., & Iwaki, G. (1990). *The final voyage of the* Challenger. Boston: Harvard Business School.

Heisenberg, W. (1958). *Physics and philosophy: The revolution in modern science*. New York: Harper and Row.

Hock, D. (1999). *Birth of the chaordic age*. San Francisco: Berrett-Koehler.

Isaacs, W. (1999). *Dialogue and the art of thinking together*. New York: Doubleday.

Janis, I. L. (1983). *Groupthink: Psychological studies of policy decisions and fiascoes* (2nd Rev. ed.). Boston: Houghton Mifflin Company.

Jaworski, J. (1996). *Synchronicity: Inner path of leadership*. San Francisco: Berrett-Koehler.

Jazz School Lucerne. (2004). Give and take: The collective conversation and musical journey. In *Picking notes out of thin air? Improvisation and its study*. Available from http://www.jsl.ch/quotes/quotes13.htm

Kotter, J. P. (1985). *Power and influence: Beyond formal authority*. New York: Free Press.

Kotter, J. P. (1996). *Leading change*. Cambridge, MA: Harvard Business School Press.

Kouzes, J. M., & Posner, B. Z. (1987). *The leadership challenge: How to get extraordinary things done in organizations*. San Francisco: Jossey-Bass.

Land, G., & Jarman, B. (1992). *Breakpoint and beyond. Mastering the future today*. New York: HarperPerennial.

Langer, E. (1989). *Mindfulness: Choice and control in everyday life*. Cambridge, MA: Perseus Books.

Laszlo, E. (1996). Subtle connections: Psi, Grof, Jung, and the quantum vacuum. *Dynamical Psychology: An International, Interdisciplinary Journal of Complex Mental Processes*. Available from http://www.goertzel.org/dynapsyc/1996/subtle.html

LeDoux, J. (1996). *The emotional brain: The mysterious underpinnings of emotional life*. New York: Simon & Schuster.

Lewin, K. (1938). *The conceptual representation and the measurement of psychological forces*. Durham, NC: Duke University Press.

Lindstrom, P. H., & Speck, M. (2004). *The principal as professional development leader*. Thousand Oaks, California: Corwin Press.

May, R. (1975). *The courage to create*. New York: Bantam.

Nelson, R. (2001). Correlation of global events with REG data: An Internet-based, nonlocal anomalies experiment. *The Journal of Parapsychology, 65*, 547–571.

Nelson, R. (2002). Coherent consciousness and reduced randomness: Correlations on September 11, 2001. *Journal of Scientific Exploration, 16*(4), 540–570.

Nelson, R. (2004). *September 11 2001: Exploratory and contextual analyses*. Available from http://noosphere.princeton.edu/terror.html

Ouchi, W. (1981). *Theory Z: How American business can meet the Japanese challenge*. Reading, MA: Addison-Wesley.

Owen, H. (1997). *Open space technology: A user's guide*. San Francisco: Berrett-Kohler.

Peck, M. S. (1987). *The different drum: Community-making and peace*. New York: Simon & Schuster.

Persinger, M. A., & Krippner, S. (1989). Dream ESP experiments and geomagnetic activity. *The Journal of the American Society for Psychical Research, 83*, 101–116.

Peters, T. (1987). *Thriving on chaos: Handbook for a management revolution*. New York: Alfred A. Knopf.

Quinn, R. E. (1996). *Deep change: Discover the leader within*. San Francisco: Jossey-Bass.

Radin, D. (2002). Exploring relationships between random physical events and mass human attention: Asking for whom the bell tolls. *Journal of Scientific Exploration, 16*(4), 533–547.

Scargle, J. D. (2002). Was there evidence of global consciousness on September 11, 2001? *Journal of Scientific Exploration, 16*(4), 571–577.

Scharmer, C. O. (2001). Self-transcending knowledge: Sensing and organizing around emerging opportunities. *Journal of Knowledge Management, 5*(2), 137–150.

Schon, D. A. (1983). *The reflective practitioner.* New York: Basic Books.

Schrage, M. (1995). *No more teams: Mastering the dynamics of creative collaboration.* New York: Doubleday.

Schwartz, R. A. (1993). *An integrated look at the modernist vision. Mathematical Connections, 1*(2).

Senge, P. (1990). *The fifth discipline: The art and practice of the learning organization.* New York: Doubleday.

Senge, P., Cambron-McCabe, N. H., Lucas, T., Kleiner, A., Dutton, J., & Smith, B. (2000). *Schools that learn: A fifth discipline fieldbook for educators, parents, and everyone who cares about education.* New York: Currency.

Sheldrake, R. (1999). *Dogs that know when their owners are coming home and other unexplained powers of animals.* New York: Three Rivers Press.

Stacey, R. D. (1992). *Managing the unknowable.* San Francisco: Jossey-Bass.

Tannen, D. (1998). *The argument culture: Moving from debate to dialogue.* New York: Ballantine.

Tuckman, B. W. (1965). Developmental sequence in small groups. *Psychological Bulletin, 63*, 384–399.

Ullman, M., & Krippner, S. (1970). *Dream studies and telepathy: An experimental approach.* New York: Parapsychology Foundation.

Von Oech, R. (1983). *A whack on the side of the head.* New York: Warner Books.

Wolfe, P. (2001). *Brain matters.* Alexandria, VA: Association for Supervision and Curriculum Development.

Yankelovich, D. (1999). *The magic of dialogue: Transforming conflict into cooperation.* New York: Simon & Schuster.

Index

NOTE: Page numbers in *italics* indicate illustrations.

CORWIN
PRESS

The Corwin Press logo—a raven striding across an open book—represents the union of courage and learning. Corwin Press is committed to improving education for all learners by publishing books and other professional development resources for those serving the field of K–12 education. By providing practical, hands-on materials, Corwin Press continues to carry out the promise of its motto: **"Helping Educators Do Their Work Better."**